I CHING

BY KERSON AND ROSEMARY HUANG

WORKMAN PUBLISHING, NEW YORK

For
Kathryn Camille
and Stephan

In preparing a new translation of the *I Ching*, we have
relied heavily on the textual interpretations of modern
scholars in the last half-century. Their insights are summa-
rized in the modern annotations to the *I Ching* by Gao
Heng contained in the following books (in Chinese) by
him, both reissued in 1968 by Zhong Hua Books, Hong
Kong:

Modern Annotation to the Old Classic Zhou Yi
Discourses on the Old Classic Zhou Yi

We acknowledge our indebtedness, and pay homage to
Gao Heng and all the scholars who have given us a fresh
and probably truer view of the *I Ching*.

Library of Congress Cataloging-in-Publication Data

Huang, Kerson, 1928–
  I ching.
  1. I ching. I. Huang, Rosemary. II. I ching.
English. 1987. III. Title.
PL2464.27H75 1987   299'.51282   86-40599
ISBN 0-89480-319-0

Cover and book design: Charles Kreloff

Workman Publishing Company, Inc.
1 West 39 Street
New York, NY 10018

Manufactured in the United States of America

CONTENTS

In the three thousand years since the I Ching was created as the court oracle of a Chinese dynasty, it has been analyzed, annotated, and embellished to such an extent that its original face has become all but unrecognizable.

The Taoists emphasized the symbolism of the hexagrams alone. Dispensing with the text altogether, they built a rich numerological system around the hexagrams which was akin to astrology. This system became the dominant influence in Chinese folk culture, and still touches the daily lives of millions of people through its role in liturgy, geomancy, life-nurturing practices, and medical theory.

The Confucians claimed the I Ching as their own, and read into the archaic and cryptic text a rigid moralistic interpretation. This was achieved through annotations and embellishments known as the Ten Wings, which became an integral part of the I Ching when Confucianism became the state creed of China during the third century.

The Taoists left the original I Ching untouched; they merely bypassed it. In contrast the Confucians came close to destroying it. They presumed themselves, and were officially certified, to be the true keepers of the I Ching, whereas the stilted prose of the Ten Wings bore no relation to the spirit and substance of the original I Ching.

The Western reader knows the I Ching chiefly through Richard Wilhelm's 1923 German translation, which was rendered into English by Cary F. Baynes.* Carl Jung used this version as a psychoanalytic tool, thereby conferring on it legitimacy, and helped make it the prophet of the counterculture of the sixties. But this conscientious and painstaking work represents a faithful rendition of the Confucian interpretation as seen through Christian eyes, and reveals little of the I Ching's original meaning.

In fact, the true face of the I Ching laid buried for two thousand years, until the passing of the Confucian state in China enabled scholars to make objective and dispassionate studies.

We now know that the text of the I Ching is a compilation of divination texts, containing folk poetry that still rhymes in modern Chinese, and historical tales that are still part of the living folklore of the Chinese people. On closer examination, an underlying philosophy emerges.

The central theme is that all things run their cycle, and no situation remains immutable. It offers hope in the depth of despair, and warns of destruction at the height of success. This is of course the philosophy of Yin, Yang, and change; but the terms are not explicitly mentioned.

Through the text runs a moral thread, which foreshadows the most noble ideals of Confucianism: A respect for the Natural Order, an esteem for self-cultivation, and a sense of social justice. Doubtless it was part of the fountainhead of Confucian thought, but a far cry from the stultifying mold it was forced into by the official Confucians.

The original text must have been compiled, weeded out and edited over a long period of time, guided by the empirical test of its effectiveness as oracle. The poetic voicing of an underlying philosophy must have been a form that emerged only after long evolution, as something essential in the making of a good oracle.

The Taoist invocation of a magical numerology is a tangential exercise independent of the original I Ching. The systematic moralization of the bureaucratic Confucians is distasteful in intention, and an act of vandalism in execution. The I Ching is simply what it was originally meant to be—an oracle.

In the modern world we perceive the cosmology of Yin and Yang as a powerful allegory rather than physical truth, the latter having been entrusted to Science. As an oracle that explores the inner cosmology of human feelings, however, the I Ching is as valid as it was two thousand years ago. The only difference is that we know the distinction between the inner cosmos and the outer, and this, paradoxically, makes an oracle more necessary and acceptable.

To the modern reader, then, there is a need for a version of the I Ching that is faithful to its original face, conveying the poetry of the lines, and the gentle philosophy of the whole. The reader may then read it for its own worth, and tailor it to an individualized interpretation. Our purpose in this new translation is to fulfill this need.

K.H.   R.H.

Marblehead, Massachusetts
February, 1987

* Wilhelm/Baynes, I Ching (Princeton University Press, 1967).

I CHING, CANON OF CHANGE

THE LEGEND

In the beginning there was nothing. The vapors that were light gathered together, and so did the vapors that were heavy. The former is called Yang, the latter is called Yin.

And thus there were two.

An early sage (some say emperor), Fuxi, whose identity and times were lost in deep antiquity, created the trigrams, figures made up of three elements that are either Yin or Yang. There are eight trigrams, and they symbolize the basic elements of a recognizable universe: Heaven, Earth, Thunder, Water, Mountain, Wind, Fire, and Lake.

And thus there were eight.

Millennia passed. Legendary dynasties rose and fell.

Some time around 2200 B.C. a great flood covered the earth. It was brought under control by Yu, who worked ceaselessly for nine years. So busy was he that "thrice he had gone past his own house without even looking in." As reward for his achievement, the emperor gave him the throne. Thus began Xia, the first hereditary dynasty in China. A thousand years later, at the end of the Shang Dynasty, King Wen of the state of Zhou stacked the trigrams on top of one another, making sixty-four hexagrams.

And thus there were sixty-four.

YIN AND YANG

Three thousand years ago in China, revolution brought down the house of Shang, and the mandate of Heaven passed to the Zhou. Thus began the great dynasty that saw the rise of Chinese philosophy and led to the development of the I Ching.

The Zhou people knew the deepest secret of the universe—that Yin and Yang are at the root of all things, and together in alternation they are the moving force of our world and all its manifestations. Yin is seen as passive, yielding, and nurturing, while Yang is active, dominating, and creative. Any circumstance, however intricate, can be described by a string of Yins and Yangs.

This idea that anything can be described in terms of only two basic elements is beautiful in its simplicity and forms the foundation from which the I Ching was constructed.

YIN

YANG

TRIGRAMS AND HEXAGRAMS

By putting together three lines, Yin or Yang, in all possible combinations, eight trigrams were formed and were used to represent the eight basic elements.

HEAVEN

EARTH

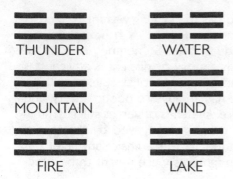

THUNDER WATER

MOUNTAIN WIND

FIRE LAKE

With these eight elements as building blocks, a higher level of representation was achieved by stacking trigrams upon trigrams, creating the sixty-four hexagrams.

Each hexagram has an opening text called "the judgment," and each of the six lines of a hexagram also has its own text. The judgment describes the general idea of the hexagram as a whole, and the individual lines refer to specific elements in the development of the central idea. This structure allows both a general reading and a more specific assessment of the meanings of the moment. The hexagrams and the text together comprise the I Ching, which served as the court oracle of the Zhou Dynasty. The character I (pronounced "ee") means "change," and Ching means "canon." Thus, I Ching means "Canon of Change."

CHANGE

The concept of change comes from the basic nature of Yin and Yang, which are always changing into each other. When Yin holds sway for too long, it "grows old" and renews itself by changing into Yang, and vice versa. When a given line in a hexagram changes, it turns the original hexagram into a new one. Thus each line has a dynamic quality, which drives the static hexagram into motion.

By associating a hexagram with a given moment in time or a particular human situation and focusing on this dynamic aspect of the hexagram, we can derive a symbolic reading of the portents. The changing, or "old," lines relate directly to the situation or question posed, and the hexagram that is created when these lines renew themselves indicates the direction of the changes. Thus the I Ching assesses both the current moment and the dynamic forces of the future, already implicit in the present.

THE TEXT

The specific text evolved as the I Ching was formalized as a tool for divination, or oracle, but each hexagram expresses its own individual style. Sometimes it gives an omen; sometimes it tells a story or dispenses advice. It is full of historical references, some recognizable, but others long lost. The language has an austere poetic quality, and despite its archaic nature, snatches of verses still rhyme in modern Chinese. The message conveyed by the text is often obscure, partly due to the archaic language, but mainly because these judgments were meant to be oracular pronouncements.

In later times, after court soothsayers were no longer used, the I Ching was taken over by the followers of Confucius for their own. They regarded the I Ching not as an oracle, but primarily as a guide to correct conduct according to what they called the Natural Order, the way of all things as revealed by Nature's working. Voluminous addenda known as the Ten Wings were added, and these have been considered an inseparable part of the I Ching for generations. In reality, however, the Ten Wings sprang from a much later era and are in no way relevant to the spirit and purpose of the original I Ching.

Whether by ignorance or design, the Ten Wings have consistently twisted all the historical tales in the I Ching into just another admonishment on observing one's proper place. Instead of clarifying the I Ching, they actually disguise its true face, thereby diminishing its power and significance. In the present translation, we clip the Wings altogether and restore the I Ching to an unblemished state.

A TOUR OF HISTORY WITH THE I CHING

TELLING STORIES

History occupies an important place in the Chinese consciousness. The common people love to recount personalities and events of the past and relate them to their present lives. It is indicative of the grass-roots character of the I Ching that it, too, likes to tell historical stories. Some of them can be immediately recognized as the very ones still in the living lore today. Many stories that were long considered obscure philosophical allegories turn out to be references to historical tales, discovered only recently with the help of modern scholarship. Still others are revealed as fragments of lost tales that can no longer be reconstructed.

The following pieces together a quick tour of ancient Chinese history through known references in the I Ching, with narrative supplied for continuity.

THE DAWN OF HISTORY

The earliest historical event mentioned in the I Ching occurred a thousand years before it, during the Xia Dynasty (ca. 2200 B.C.):

> *The rebellious cometh.*
> *Last to arrive, he meets his end.*
> (8 SUPPORT)

This refers to a famous story about Yu, founder of the dynasty, conqueror of the Great Deluge. When a particularly uppity chieftain, Fang Feng, came late to a summoned meeting, Yu used that as the pretext to have him executed.

During the middle years of the Xia Dynasty, there occurred an episode of intrigue and adventure concerning a prince born posthumously to a king in exile. It apparently inspired hexagram 38 ABANDONED, which recounts the strange experiences of an abandoned waif, with a bizarre final line:

> *The abandoned waif saw a pig in the mud,*
> *And a cart full of demons.*
> *He arched his bow at first,*
> *But finally put it down.*
> *They are not robbers, only wife grabbers.*
> *Going would be favorable if it rains.*
> (38 ABANDONED)

The saga began in the year 2119 B.C., when the Master of Archery Yoxiung usurped the throne and drove the King, Xiang, into exile. Not long after, however, Yoxiung himself was murdered by his aide, Hanju, who not only took over the throne, but also married Yoxiung's widow, who bore him two sons. One of them, named Wao, was so strong that he could "navigate a boat on land" (presumably by dragging it). Hanju sent this gorilla of a son to kill King Xiang in his place of exile. The pregnant queen of King Xiang escaped to the state of Yoying, where she gave birth to Shao Kang (Kang the Younger), who grew up to be Master of Husbandry in his adopted state.

Upon learning the whereabouts of the murdered King's son, Hanju sent assassins to kill him. Shao Kang got wind of the plan and escaped. He wandered about for some time and finally settled down in the state of Yoyu. He became master of the local king's kitchen and thwarted an attempt to poison the king through his food. In gratitude, the king gave him the hands of his two daughters in marriage.

After a lapse of some twenty years, the double usurper Hanju was finally overthrown by loyal forces, and Shao Kang regained the throne that was rightfully his.

The Xia Dynasty ended in 1783 B.C., when its bad emperor, Jie, was toppled from the throne by the good Lord Tang. So began the great Shang Dynasty, which heralded the dawn of recorded history.

THE GREAT BRONZE AGE

The Shang Dynasty and the Zhou, which later replaced it, were particularly important for the I Ching. The Zhou created it as their own oracle, and Shang figures prominently in it, being the center of power and culture that the Zhou had looked up to.

The Shang Dynasty lasted almost seven hundred years. It was the political and cultural center of a China made up of loosely federated kingdoms. The I Ching deferentially refers to Shang as "the Great Kingdom" (64 UNFULFILLMENT). It was the mecca of students from neighboring states. Calligraphy, the highest art form in traditional China, was already well developed. It perfected the technique of bronze casting and bequeathed us with those mystically austere bronze vessels, which have not been surpassed as works of art.

The Shang capital was located in the basin of the capricious Yellow River, which periodically changed course, sweeping over vast areas. Thus, floods were an ever-present threat, causing the Shang capital to be moved eight times in its history. These circumstances were important to the relationship between Shang and its neighbor, Zhou, as noted in the I Ching:

> Water laps at the King's house.
> It's safe.
>
>   (59 FLOWING)

> On the road, the Duke got the news, agreed,
> And assisted in moving the Capital.
>
> (42 INCREASE)

The last quote records how Zhou, then a vassal state of Shang, assisted in the moving of the Shang capital. The same hexagram goes on to imply that, by gaining Shang's trust, Zhou set the stage for overthrowing Shang. The events referred to very likely occurred in 1388 B.C., when the Shang capital made its final move to An Yang, where archaeologists have unearthed entire bronze foundries and the fabulous oracle bones that we will discuss more fully later.

The I Ching most likely had its roots in the divination traditions of the Shang. The Shang people deified their ancestors, to whom periodic offerings were required, with the proper ceremony. These rites were among the most important duties of the king.

Of the early ancestors of the Shang people, only three were considered important enough to merit the title of "High Ancestor," and they were honored with especially elaborate sacrifices. Among them was Wang Hai (Prince Hai), who figures prominently in the I Ching, though it is not clear why he in particular is referred to so frequently.

Prince Hai (ca. 2000 B.C.) was a clever, enterprising, and restless man who left his home to travel to the Kingdom of Yi to raise cattle and seek his fortune:

> Little, little traveler,
> Leaves his home to wander,
> Courting disaster.
>
> (56 THE TRAVELER)

There Prince Hai encountered mysterious conspiracies against him. He had a flourishing flock of sheep, but somehow lost it:

> He lost his sheep in the Kingdom of Yi.
> No regrets.
>
> (34 GREAT INJURY)

He then raised oxen and invented the ox yoke to put them to work in the field. There was an attempt to burn him to death in his house, from which he was able to escape only because a mysterious rap on his bed roused him:

Hitting the bed with the foot.
The dream bodes ill.
(23 Loss)

His luck did not hold out for long, however. The local King, Mianshen, who may have been behind all the conspiracies, finally killed him and took his oxen:

A bird's nest is burning.
The traveler first laughs then weeps.
He lost his oxen at the Kingdom of Yi.
Disaster.
(56 THE TRAVELER)

Prince Hai's death was eventually avenged by his son Wei, who, with the assistance of a neighboring state, attacked Yi and killed Mianshen.

A century after Prince Hai, his descendant Lord Tang overthrew the Xia and founded the Shang Dynasty. Lord Tang took pains to project a public image of diligence and humanity. On his bath basin was inscribed the famous maxim:

Renew yourself today,
And another day,
And each and every day.

One day, when he saw hunters closing in on their prey with nets from all four sides, he ordered the nets removed on three of the sides. In his dominion, he declared, "only willing animals shall be taken." When people in the neighboring states heard about this, they all praised him for his compassion, which "benefited even the wild beasts." The I Ching probably had this incident in mind when it wryly commented:

The gentleman loosened the rope.
Good for him.
The common folks got the punishment.
(40 LETTING LOOSE)

JOU THE TERRIBLE

In 1151 B.C., the last Shang emperor, Jou the Terrible, ascended to the throne. To this day, his name is synonymous with "debauched tyrant." An intelligent and powerful man, he "fought wild beasts with his bare hands." He used to throw wild orgies for three thousand people. Men and women would run around naked, gorging themselves in a forest whose leaves were made of meat and, to the beat of a drum, dip their heads in unison to drink, "like cows," from a lake of wine.

Most unforgivable of all, he pandered to the every whim of Taji, his beautiful but petulant queen. One day, she wondered whether what they said of Jou's uncle, Prince Bigan, was true, that his heart had seven chambers instead of the usual four, and that's why he was so wise. To satisfy her curiosity, Jou killed Bigan and took his heart out for examination. Another uncle, the Prime Minister Jizi, was thrown into prison when he admonished Jou on his excesses; he escaped execution only by feigning madness.

Meanwhile, the state of Zhou had gained influence among all the vassal states because of its wise ruler, King Wen (The Humane King). It was said that all the states would bring their disputes before King Wen to be settled because they could always be assured of a wise and fair arbitration. Jou's father, Emperor Yi, had given his daughter in marriage to King Wen. The I Ching noted the occasion through a sharp reporter's eye:

Emperor Yi betrothed his daughter.
With her niece as consort.
(11 PEACE)

Emperor Yi gave his daughter in marriage.
The Princess is not as beautiful as her consort.
(54 THE MARRYING MAIDEN)

The bride seemed to be upstaged by her niece, the consort (concubine). Small wonder. She eventually mothered King Wen's heir, King Wu.

King Wen's reputation and influence made Jou jealous. On one of King Wen's tributary visits to the Shang court, Jou threw him in prison, where he was confined for seven years. While in prison, King Wen reflected on Yin and Yang and the trigrams and had the idea of stacking a trigram upon a trigram to form a hexagram, symbolizing a higher level of diversification. He gave names to the sixty-four possible hexagrams and attached to each a text to convey its attribute.

The body of text that King Wen wrote is called Guazi (Hexagram text), the skeleton of the I Ching. (In Chinese, both trigram and hexagram are called Gua. Guazi means "Gua text.")

The release of King Wen was eventually arranged by brib-
ing Jou with beautiful women, fine horses, and rare
animals. Jou was so pleased with the presents ("Any one of
these would have sufficed") that he even granted King
Wen the right to bear arms against his neighboring states.
These events are referred to in the I Ching:

THE MANDATE OF HEAVEN

> *Someone is proffering a tortoise shell.*
> *Worth ten double cowries.*
> *It cannot be refused.*
> *Everlasting good omen.*
> *The King makes offerings to God.*
> *Good fortune.*
>
> (42 INCREASE)

> *Imprisoned first, then set free,*
> *The King makes offerings at West Mountain.*
>
> (17 THE CHASE)

> *The King offers sacrifice at Mount Qi.*
> *All goes well. No troubles.*
>
> (46 ASCENDANCE)

King Wen had able sons. Among them, Marquis Kang
was an especially able warrior:

> *Marquis Kang presented a herd of horses,*
> *The spoils of three victories in one day.*
>
> (35 ADVANCE)

Another son, the wise and learned Duke Zhou, inherited
the secret of the hexagrams. The noblest of them all, son
of Taisi, the consort mentioned before, he succeeded King
Wen as King Wu, the Valiant King.

The plan to overthrow Jou the Terrible was long in
planning. King Wen had taken advantage of the right to
bear arms granted him by Jou to bring his immediate
neighbors in line. Then he sought out the wise hermit Lu
Wang, known to later ages as the Old Master Jiang, to be
his right-hand man.

Lu Wang had spent his idle time fishing, with a
straight hook. When asked about this seemingly futile exercise, he answered, "What I am after is not fish." He
inspired the romantic ideal of the philosopher hermit,
who eschews the material glories of the world to wait for
the call of a truly noble cause. As the I Ching admonishes:

> *Serve not the mighty.*
> *Keep your goals lofty.*
> (18 WORK)

King Wen died without taking action against Jou. His successor, King Wu, made Lu Wan his Chief-of-Staff, and held a military exercise on the banks of the River Meng. Eight hundred heads of states came to meet him and urge him to move against the evil Jou. Just then, a white fish leapt into King Wu's boat. King Wu saw it as a warning that Jou was still strong, for white is the color of Shang. He returned home and continued to make preparations for another two years.

The reckoning came just before dawn one February day, in the year 1122 B.C. King Wu's call for a revolution was answered by all the neighboring states, who came forth with four thousand chariots. Before the joint forces assembled in the field of Mu, he delivered a historic speech that was preserved for posterity in the Book of Records.

King Wu began by citing an old adage about a house corrupted by "a hen that crows." He vowed to fulfill the mandate of Heaven to deliver the people from the clutches of tyranny. And he charged the soldiers, "Onward! Be as tigers, as bears. He who falls behind shall be executed." The I Ching takes note of this historic occasion:

> *On the day of the public gathering,*
> *A new order is proclaimed.*
> (49 REVOLUTION)

Jou met the revolutionary forces with an army of seven hundred thousand. However, it was a ragtag army with no will to fight, and most of the soldiers went over to King Wu. As the I Ching commented;

> *None will rally*
> *Some will attack.*
> *If there is no determination in the heart,*
> *Disaster will befall.*

> (42 INCREASE)

And disaster did befall the evil Jou. Conceding defeat, he retreated to the Deer Pavilion, scene of his numerous past orgies. There, clasping to his bosom his priceless jade collection, Jou set himself on fire and burned to death. King Wu drove up in a chariot and shot

Jou's body three times with arrows. Then he beheaded Jou's corpse with a yellow ax, and hanged the head on a white banner for all to see. He proclaimed himself Emperor and appointed his brother Duke Zhou as Prime Minister.

To show that peace was restored, King Wu "released the war steeds to the east slope of Mount Hua, sent oxen grazing in the plain of Taolin, gathered all weapons, and dispersed the army. Thus it was made known to all under Heaven that force shall never be used again." The I Ching rejoiced with characteristic guardedness:

> Shang is vanquished.
> Some things are possible.
> (2 EARTH)

Jizi was released from prison but did not wish to serve under Zhou rule. With five thousand followers, he migrated to a peninsula in the northeast and founded the Kingdom of Chosen, also known as Korea. There is a tomb in Pyongyang bearing his name. The life of Jizi inspired hexagram 36 THE CRYING PHEASANT.

Thus began the Zhou Dynasty, which lasted a glorious eight centuries, spawning in its waning years the Golden Age of the philosophers, including Laozi and Confucius.

THE ORACLE OF CHANGE

Duke Zhou was a wise and humble public servant. To encourage people to come to him with ideas, he always kept his door open. It was said that in his eagerness to welcome guests, he usually interrupted a meal three times by spitting out the food, and got out of a bath three times, clutching his wet hair.

Some five centuries later, Confucius would tout him as the model statesman. In his own declining years, when his ideas of statecraft had failed to gain acceptance, Confucius lamented, "How I must be getting old! It's been so long since Duke Zhou came to my dreams."

Duke Zhou breathed life into the lines of King Wen's hexagrams by writing a text to convey their attributes. Together with the judgments written by King Wen, this constitutes Yi (Change), or Zhou Yi (The Book of Change of Zhou). It is now known by the name I Ching.

Rules were formalized to use the Zhou Yi for divination, which was entrusted to an official court oracle. The Dynasty was now properly launched, for it had been registered with Heaven.

The history could end here but for the fact that Confucius was yet to leave his imprint, which gave the I Ching the impact it has had on Chinese culture for centuries.

3

THE LEGACY OF CONFUCIUS

Sima Qian, the great historian of the second century B.C., noted that every five hundred years a great sage takes center stage. From great antiquity, philosopher kings and sages rose to mark new eras in five-hundred-year intervals down to Duke Zhou. Five hundred years after Duke Zhou came Confucius, sage of sages.

All dynasties end, sooner or later. While Shang ended spectacularly, Zhou just faded away. By the time Confucius was born, in 550 B.C., the local lords had become so powerful and independent that the court of Zhou had merely titular significance. The dominions of the lords were in reality separate nations, each with its own way of government, war, and diplomacy.

It was a lawless time, a time when a criminal wanted in one dukedom could flee to a neighboring one and become its prime minister overnight. It was also a time of great intellectual ferment, for which the phrase "a hundred flowers bloom, a hundred schools contend" was originally coined.

The two major schools of thought, the Taoist and the Confucian, both longed to bring the world back to an ancient "Golden Era." Each school, however, painted the ideal very differently.

Laozi, whom the Taoists claimed as founding father, held that government was at the root of all evil. According to Laozi, the ideal world of ancient times consisted of "small countries with small populations, which had no intercourse with one another. Thus, newfangled inventions, even if made, could find no application." As a political goal, this obviously did not have a ghost of a chance, but the personal philosophy behind it—accomplishment by inaction, activity through passivity—had a profound impact on Chinese thought.

Confucius, on the other hand, looked back to the times of the ancient emperors (which predated the Xia Dynasty) as a Golden Era, when rulers were compassionate and just and subjects were decorous and loyal. This ideal condition was made possible by the maintenance of a proper social order, in which each person fulfilled the duty of his station. To achieve that felicitous state, people had to be inculcated with a desire for learning and self-cultivation. His disciples recorded his views as follows, in The Great Learning:

> In ancient times, he who wished to let his virtue shine over all under Heaven must first govern his state well. To govern the state well, he must first unify his clan. To unify the clan, he must first cultivate himself. To cultivate himself, his heart must be in the right place. For the heart to be in the right place, he must first have a sincere purpose. To have a sincere purpose, he must first acquire knowledge. The way to acquire knowledge is to study the nature of things.
>
> When the nature of things is understood, knowledge will be gained. When knowledge is gained, a sincere purpose can be set. When a sincere purpose is set, the heart can find the right

*place. When the heart is in the right place, the self
can be cultivated. When the self is cultivated, the
clan can be unified. When the clan is unified, the
state can be well-governed. When the state is
well-governed, order can be brought to all under
heaven.*

*For the emperor and common man alike,
self-cultivation is the key.*

Thus, according to Confucius, there is a hierarchical
external social order, which is mirrored in a hierarchical
internal personal order. The great rulers were successful
because they were able to project their internal order
onto the external world.

Confucius allegedly held the Yi in the highest esteem,
as a perfect expression of the Natural Order, which fur-
nishes a basis for the hierarchy of the inner personal
order. The progression of personal development, from
learning the basics to bringing order to the world, can be
likened to the development of grand structures out of the
basic Yin and Yang. In his later years, he read the Yi so
often, it was said, that the leather binding had to be thrice
replaced. "Grant me a few more years to study the Yi,"
he said. "I should then be able to avoid grave errors."

To expound his views on the relationship between
the I Ching and human affairs, Confucius was said to have
written the Ten Wings, essays appended to the original Yi
of King Wen and Duke Zhou. (We shall see, however, that
the Ten Wings could not have been the work of Confucius. Neither do they serve the Yi well.)

Confucius kept a kind of editorialized chronicle of the
events of his era, The Annals of Spring and Autumn, in
which he sought to distinguish right from wrong through a
few incisively chosen words. It was said that these words
struck terror in the hearts of all troublemakers. The years
covered by the Annals (722–480 B.C.) have since been
known as the "Era of Spring and Autumn." The laconic
Annals were expanded by contemporary historians into
full histories, containing records of numerous I Ching
readings by the rulers of the time. We shall quote a few
examples in a later chapter.

DEATH OF A QILIN

True to their own philosophies, Laozi and Confucius reacted quite differently to the turmoils of the time. Laozi simply got on the back of a blue ox one day and headed west. When he was about to cross the Great Wall to leave China, the keeper of one of the gates saw a "purple aura" approaching from the east and knew that a great man was coming. He greeted and entertained Laozi and took down by dictation the Daode Jing (Tao Teh Ching), which has become the bible of Taoism. Laozi got back on his blue ox and rode into the sunset, never to be heard from again.

Confucius, on the other hand, stumped the country to preach his vision of the ideal society. He acquired a following of three thousand disciples, but not a single ruler was among them. One day, someone killed a strange unicorn-like beast in the field, attracting a crowd of curious onlookers. Confucius went to investigate, recognized that it was a qilin, symbol of the Golden Era, and uttered a lament heard down the ages:

> O, Qilin! You belong to the Golden Age,
> With the birds of paradise.
> What misguided mission
> Has sent you to our time?

That day, Confucius entered the last line in his Annals. He died soon after, a disappointed man. It was to be another five hundred years before his ideals became universally accepted.

HOW CHINA GOT HER NAME

The Iron Age came. Weapons became sharper. Zhou finally disappeared, and the Era of Warring States began, which ended when one state gobbled up all others. For the first time, the land was unified under one centralized state, which took on the name of the conquering kingdom, Qin, transliterated into the tongues of remote western countries as "China." It was 221 B.C.

The first emperor of Qin called himself The First Emperor. His son was to be The Second Emperor, and so forth, until The Ten Thousandth, and beyond. In a burst of exuberance, he reportedly built a palace that covered a hundred miles and a mausoleum under an artificial mountain, which, among other wonders, contained a giant relief map of China with quicksilver running in the rivers. As we know for a fact, he ordered an army of six thousand life-sized clay soldiers buried underground, in battle formation, to guard his tomb. And, of course, he completed the Great Wall.

But what he really wanted was to live forever. A wizard, Xushi, promised to bring him the herb of immortality from a fabled island in the East Sea, where the sun rises. All he required was a fleet staffed with three thousand boys and as many girls. Xushi went on his mission and was never heard from again. However, there is a tomb in Japan bearing his name.

The First Emperor had no use for Confucius and Natural Order. Had he not forged a nation through blood and iron alone? To suppress idle pursuit, which might endanger the throne, he had three hundred alleged Confucian scholars buried alive and ordered all books burned, except those on medicine and other useful subjects. The I Ching was spared because as a book on divination it was deemed useful.

I CHING ENSHRINED

The Qin Dynasty lasted a mere fifteen years. After the death of the First Emperor, uprisings broke out all over the land. By elimination and merger, there quickly emerged two major forces vying for the throne: Chu and Han. Chu had the irresistibly romantic combination of Macho Hero, Thoroughbred Steed, and Great Beauty. In contrast, the leader of Han was a boorish small-town bailiff. But Han won. Chu's final defeat came when its retreating army was pushed against the Black River by the Han forces, who sang folk songs of Chu through the night, prompting many desertions among the demoralized and homesick Chu soldiers. The end has been portrayed in a famous Peking opera, Power Lord Bids Farewell to His Lady. Generations of theatergoers have shed tears over the dramatic final act, when Great Beauty performs the last sword dance to the beat of muffled drums for Macho Hero and kills herself at his feet. Whereupon our Hero slits his own throat with a sword, and his body tumbles into the Black River.

The Han Dynasty was proclaimed in 207 B.C. It instituted a system of civil examinations as the door to public service. Under the great Emperor Wu (The Valiant Emperor), who reigned from 140 to 86 B.C., the system was completed. Confucianism was declared state creed, and the I Ching, including the Ten Wings, took its place among the Confucian Classics, thirteen in number, which had to be mastered by all who aspired to state office. The world's first and largest bureaucracy was born.

Thus, five hundred years after Confucius, the I Ching became enshrined, not as Oracle, but as Teacher. Its original function as a vehicle for divination was now considered secondary. Instead, it was revered as an expression of the deepest secret of Nature: the unceasing alternation between Yin and Yang that makes the world go round. It was to be the inspiration for a life in harmony with Nature.

The imperial court no longer maintained an official soothsayer. The signs of Heaven remained a serious concern; but they were now read by the Imperial Astronomer, who was the father of Sima Qian.

Sima Qian witnessed this watershed of history in his lifetime. He wrote the monumental Records of History, the first systematic history of China from legendary beginnings to his time, emphasizing personalities and events that figured in the long sweep of cultural development. He had intended it as a kind of time capsule, "to be secreted in a sacred mountain, preserved for a later generation." Much of what we know about ancient Chinese history, including that of the I Ching, came from this work.

And thus did Sima Qian became the sage of his era, five hundred years after Confucius—a role known to himself and posterity, but not to his contemporaries.

THE CONFUCIAN HERITAGE

No single person has had more influence on the culture of China, and by extension of Japan, Korea, and other nations of East Asia, than Confucius. He was a modest man, by his own estimate a failure in his lifetime. Qin, the power that initially unified China, did not believe in his teachings, nor in those of the Taoists, but opted instead for those of the Legalists, a hard-nosed aproach to the acquisition and management of centralized power.

Once political power was securely entrenched, however, the ruler needed something more transcendental than cost-effectiveness on which to base his rule, and he found it in the Confucian concept of Natural Order.

The Confucian ideal was appealing because it appeared to be eminently reasonable, and it also had the strong advantage of having deep cultural roots. In the original text of the I Ching, we find a humane pragmatism, an earnest work ethic, a sense of social justice, and a respect for the natural way that were hallmarks of the Confucian outlook. These values could not have been the I Ching's creation, but must have come in turn from a still-older tradition, of which the I Ching was synthesizer.

Once institutionalized, Confucianism inevitably became standardized, sanitized, and sterilized. The I Ching, too, had to be repackaged, and the Ten Wings accomplished that. They were of course attributed to Confucius himself, but by content and style they were clearly products of a much later age.

As the name implies, the Ten Wings consists of ten essays, which vary considerably in quality. The ones that discourse on the general philosophy of the I Ching make for good reading, although they impute to the I Ching more than what was there originally. The following is a sampling of more memorable passages:

Heaven was above, Earth below: Thus the universe took form. The lofty and the lowly segregated: Thus the correct positions were established. Motion and rest became regulated: Thus the active and the passive found their roles. The likes congregated, and all things divided into classes: Thus good and evil arose. Signs were displayed in heaven, and shapes appeared on Earth: Thus change was manifest. The active and the passive massaged each other. The eight trigrams excited one another. Driven by thunder and lightning, nurtured by wind and rain, with the rotations of the Sun and the Moon, with the seasonal alternation of cold and heat, the pure Yang became the male, and the pure Yin the female . . .

A Yin. A Yang. That is the Tao. The compassionate finds in it, humanity. The intellectual finds in it, reason. The common people are daily immersed in it unawares. Thus the way of the sages is subtle . . .

These sophisticated discourses are a far cry from the primitive and powerful poetry of the original I Ching. Whereas in the original the underlying philosophy is brought out gently through examples, morality is explicitly prescribed in these essays. The Ten Wings weave a theory of a hierarchy in Nature, which not coincidentally reflects the hierarchy in the Confucian ideal of society.

Other parts of the Ten Wings do not make much sense. This is especially true of The Image, which is truly destructive of the original face of the I Ching, for it is interlaced line by line with the original text. The content is a kind of "official speak" that is neither I Ching nor Confucius.

To give an example, let us see what The Image has to say about two selected lines from 59 FLOWING. We shall display the lines in the form one usually finds in standard editions. The original text is immediately followed by The Image, which is incomprehensible unless annotated by some great Confucian scholar. Here we use the famous annotation of Kung Yingda of the Tang Dynasty:

▬▬ ▬▬ **3** *Water laves the body, no regrets.*
The Image: Water laves the body, for the mind is outwardly directed.
Note: Six in the third place can lave its body, because it is inside, and responds to nine at the top. That's why it is outwardly directed.

▬▬▬▬▬ **5** *Sweating profusely, wailing loudly. Water laps at the King's House. It's safe.*
The Image: The King's house is safe, because it is in the rightful place.
Note: Nine in the fifth place is the King's proper place.

We can see that the text is really quite straightforward and spontaneous, but the so-called Image is pure gobbledegook, and the annotations only make it worse. Yet none would dare openly declare that "the Emperor has no clothes," for in imperial China the Ten Wings were made part of the I Ching, and required reading for the aspiring mandarin, who had to pass the civil examinations. And thus the original face of the I Ching laid buried for two millennia, until resurrected by modern scholarship and fresh points of view made possible by the passing of the Confucian state.

There was the true Confucius, grand synthesizer of a Utopian past, who held Natural Order in reverence, valued self-cultivation, and approached the world with humane pragmatism. His values were the distillations of the best of ancient traditions, which still shine through the essential I Ching, when stripped of all the encrustations of bureaucratic prose. Through Confucius, even the institutionalized one, these values have become deeply ingrained in the Chinese way. The dynastic rulers of China, in this instance, did him justice by honoring him as The Great Teacher.

4

MEANING OF THE I CHING

HEXAGRAM PATTERNS

A question of special fascination to many students of the I Ching has been whether the arrangement of hexagrams conveys a hidden message. The answer seems to be no.

The sixty-four hexagrams are given in this book in the so-called "King Wen order." It consists of a sequence of thirty-two conjugate pairs, in which one hexagram can be obtained from the other by standing it upside down. The eight hexagrams made by doubling the trigrams are exceptions to the rule, for they look the same upside down as they do right side up. These are grouped into mirrored pairs instead, in which one member is gotten from the other by interchanging the Yin and Yang lines.

The first pair of hexagrams is HEAVEN-EARTH, which seems natural enough. The last pair turns out to be FUL-FILLMENT-UNFULFILLMENT, in that order. The literal translation of the names are "After Crossing" and "Not Yet Across," referring especially to crossing a river. Their placement at the end is doubtless a deliberate irony, a comment on the elusiveness of success or the unattainability of perfection.

Apart from the above there is no obvious formula. Of course the Ten Wings, which have an answer to everything, contain an essay explaining the grand vision expressed in the King Wen arrangement; but it sounds like a press secretary explaining an executive order and does not inspire confidence.

As we shall mention later, there is an alternative "Fuxi order," which is simple and transparent; but none of the standard editions use it.

In a similar vein, there does not seem to be a systematic correlation between the Yin-Yang structure of a hexagram and its name. There are examples of obvious symbolism, such as the pair LOSS-RETURN shown in this illustration:

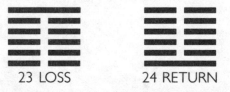

23 LOSS   24 RETURN

The first of the pair depicts a lonely Yang at the top, the last stage of development, about to turn into a retiring Yin. This symbolizes the end of a regime, hence "loss." The second describes the opposite situation, in which a youthful Yang begins to sprout from the roots, ready to extend its influence upward to turn the Yin lines into vigorous Yangs. It symbolizes renewal, hence "return."

As shown in the following illustration, MODESTY is sensibly symbolized by Mountain beneath Earth, for a mountain normally sits on top of the earth.

15 MODESTY

EARTH

OVER

MOUNTAIN

There are cases in which the name seems to be inspired by the picture presented by the hexagram, but one cannot be sure. The principles used in naming hexagrams were probably as varied as those used in designing the Chinese characters: pictographic, symbolic, metaphoric, and so forth.

I CHING AS POETRY

In the I Ching each hexagram stands as a poem. Its impact is heightened by the hexagram form, much as the effectiveness of the classical arts is enhanced by an accepted structure.

The poetic aspect of the I Ching, however, has been obscured by the Ten Wings. How can you enjoy poetry if every line is followed by government regulations on how to read it? Once the parasitic vine is torn out, however, the poetry of the symbolism and imagery becomes apparent to even a cursory reader.

Conscious use of literary devices occurs frequently. For example in 2 EARTH the metrical scheme spans all six lines of the hexagram. In the following, the words that rhyme in the original Chinese text are not italicized; unfortunately, we are not able to reproduce the effect in the English translation:

1 *Treading on* frost. . . .
2 *Straight and* square. . . .
3 Shang *is vanquished.* . . .
4 *A closed* bag. . . .
5 *A yellow* robe. . . .
6 *The dragons fight in the field.*
   Their blood runs black and yellow.
                    (2 EARTH)

The following was clearly calculated for effect:

Expelled.
Returned.
Burned.
Died.
Abandoned.
   (30 FIRE)

The starkness and power stand out in the context of the other lines of the hexagram. The original Chinese text is dramatized by exclamatory sounds after each word.

There are snatches of rhymed verse in the style of the Book of Poems, an anthology of folk and court poetry from ancient times compiled by Confucius. A standard device was the "leading image" that sets the mood for what is to come, as in the famous love song that opens the Book of Poems:

> *Guan-guan cries the kingfisher*
> *On the island in the river.*
> *There is a pretty maiden*
> *That I am yearning after.*

Compare this with the following from the I Ching:

> *An egret sings in the shade.*
> *Its young harmonizing.*
> *I have a good wine,*
> *For you to share.*
> 　　　　(61 SINCERITY)

> *Thick clouds and no rain*
> *From my west field cometh.*
> *The duke went shooting,*
> *And got the bird in a cave.*
> 　　　(62 SMALL EXCESS)

It is amusing to observe that the official Confucians also attempted an assassination of the Book of Poems. The love song quoted above was explained as a poem about the "virtues of King Wen and his Queen."

Some passages of the I Ching echo the concern with social justice found in the Book of Poems, as in the following example:

> *I fell the lumber*
> *Right by the river.*
> *O, how clear the rippling water!*
> *You never worked the land.*
> *Whence came the grain in the yard?*
> *Ah, a gentleman true*
> *Takes only his due.*

Compare the following sentiments in the I Ching:

> *Refusing a fat plum,*
> *The gentleman gains a carriage.*
> *The common man loses his house.*
> 　　　　　(23 LOSS)

The gentleman loosened the rope.
Good for him.
The common folks got the punishment.

(40 LETTING LOOSE)

This may well be folk poetry of the time that found its way into the I Ching.

I CHING AS PHILOSOPHY

The diverse hexagrams in the I Ching build up to a unifying philosophy, though not the rigid doctrine of the state Confucians. The main theme is that Yin and Yang alternate in an unending sequence; an extreme situation must change to make room for opposite elements. However, though Yin and Yang are part of the symbolism of the hexagrams, you search the text in vain for these words, or even for "change."

A hexagram generally follows the development of an idea or situation, from its inception in the first line to the ultimate fate in the last line. The first line generally sets the mood. The successive lines describe the unfolding of the situation, and the last line warns of overstepping the proper bounds. There is, however, considerable variation from this scheme. As in the ordering and the naming of hexagrams, there is no set formula. What makes the I Ching interesting, in fact, is that every hexagram is in some manner structurally unique.

The basic pattern is most clearly and forcefully expressed in the opening hexagram, HEAVEN, of pure Yang, where we follow the dragon's progress:

1 *The dragon is hibernating . . .*
2 *The dragon is seen in the fields . . .*
3 *A gentleman works hard all day . . .*
4 *The dragon is sometimes leaping in the pool . . .*
5 *The dragon is flying in the sky . . .*
6 *The dragon is stranded in the shallows . . .*

(1 HEAVEN)

The dragon is a symbol of power, strength, and creativity. It takes careful nurturing to bring it to full power. Eventually, however, the power wanes, for nothing is forever, and all things run their cycle, only to begin anew.

It is probably by design that the theme so clearly

brought out in HEAVEN is all but unrecognizable in EARTH, of pure Yin. All the lines participate in an overall metrical scheme, as we showed earlier, but their meanings are far from clear. From frost underfoot to the final cosmic battle between dragons, the lines can fit any number of inter-pretations, or none at all. Reticence and obscurity is the theme.

Between the two extremes of clarity and obscurity exemplified by HEAVEN and EARTH, all other hexagrams fall within, having varying degrees of clarity. Generally an ini-tially discouraging situation finds reprieve at the end, whereas an exuberant mood, as in I HEAVEN, gets slapped down at the end. The point is made that a ray of hope never dies in the depth of despair, while victory sows its own seed of defeat.

The development of the theme often uses parts of the human body as metaphor, progressing from the foot to the head. An interesting one is 23 LOSS, in which the idea of loss is expressed only obliquely, through reference to Prince Hai's loss of his sheep, and eventually his oxen and his life. We relive the terrifying scene when the Prince escaped death at the hands of an unknown arsonist, thanks to a mysterious rap on his bed that roused him:

1 *Hitting the bed with the foot . . .*
2 *Hitting the bed with the knee . . .*
3 *Hit it . . .*
4 *Hitting the bed with the shoulder . . .*
5 *Using a eunuch as servant . . .*
6 *Refusing a plum . . .*

(23 LOSS)

The unremitting terror, however, is somewhat alleviated at the end. The fifth line refers to a helpful servant Prince Hai found after recovering from a loss. The last line might refer to a story that has been lost, but it does not fore-bode disaster.

There is a moral thread running through the I Ching that hews quite closely to the later Confucian ethics, which explains why Confucius found the I Ching of such great interest. There is also a hardheadedness that re-minds one of Confucian pragmatism. This is of course no coincidence, for Confucius formed his ideals by distilling what was best from what he perceived as an ancient Golden Era.

Witness the third line from HEAVEN:

The gentleman works hard all day,
And keeps alerts at night.
In peril, safe.

(1 HEAVEN)

Compare this with the following from the Confucian Analects:

Zengzi said, "Each day I examine myself thrice:
"Have I been faithful in serving others?
"Have I been honest with my friends?
"Have I reviewed the Master's lessons?"

Virtue is touted not as an end in itself, but as a proper means to attain one's goals. This pragmatic approach, always concerned with this world rather than some other, is characteristic of Confucius, who refused to answer questions about the afterlife ("Before you understand life, how can you understand death?" he responded) or the spirits ("Before you learn to serve men, how can you serve the spirits?").

The conquest of Shang by Zhou was an important event from which morals are drawn. An overall assessment can be pieced together from different hexagrams.

Shang was the Great Country of superior wealth, but it was in moral decay. Zhou, on the other hand, saw itself as poorer materially but stronger spiritually. It sent its General Zhen to help King Wu Ding of Shang to pacify Devil's Land (forbearer of the Huns). It assisted Shang in moving its capital when floods ravaged it. For all this, Zhou gained the trust of Shang, and the way was open for Zhou, acting as the instrument of Heaven's wrath, to overthrow Shang through revolution.

The description of circumstances surrounding the disaster aid is quite specific:

1 *Favorable to start major construction . . .*
2 *Someone is proffering a tortoise shell . . .*
3 *Assistance offered at a disaster . . .*
4 *. . . The Duke . . . assisted in moving the Capital.*
5 *. . . Trust is our reward.*
6 *None will rally. Some will attack . . .*

(42 INCREASE)

The hexagram begins on a note of readiness to undertake a great project. The second line notes an opportunity that must be grasped. The head of the Zhou state agreed to assist in moving the Shang capital, and the reward is gaining Shang's trust. Finally the attack on Shang was launched.

With the above in mind, it is interesting to read MODESTY, the only hexagram in the entire I Ching in which all six lines give favorable readings:

4 *There is everything to gain*
To practice modesty.

5 *Losing wealth, on account of a neighbor.*
Attack brings success.

6 *Known for modesty.*
Auspicious to take military action,
To pacify the provinces.

(15 MODESTY)

The implication is that modesty is the best policy. One can capitalize on it to project a righteous image in taking aggressive action (which, the text is careful to point out, must be justifiable).

In sum, we see that the I Ching draws from history and folklore to weave poetry. In a single passage we may not find any specific message, but taken as a whole the book brings out the inevitability of change, the illusion of power, and the danger and reward that lurk in any situation. Locally it is poetry; globally it is philosophy.

As originally conceived, though, the I Ching was intended as neither poetry nor philosophy. It was an oracle. The text must have been gathered from various sources, weeded out, and edited over long periods of time, during which its effectiveness as an oracle was tested. However, the poetic voicing of an underlying philosophy could not have been accidental, but must have been discovered through experience to be essential in the making of a good oracle.

THE MANY FACES OF THE I CHING

The I Ching is different things to different people. The visual impact of the symbolism, the implicit philosophy, and the imagery in the lines are all open to personal interpretation and varied associations.

Officialdom in dynastic China had chosen to focus on the moralistic aspect of the I Ching and de-emphasize its original role as oracle. But the state Confucians were not content with merely pointing out the implicit moral message in the I Ching. They wanted to "derive" the I Ching, line by line, from a unified principle base on Yin, Yang, and change. A systematic effort to do so was undertaken by scholars of the Han dynasty (206 B.C. to A.D. 25). They dissected the hexagrams in different ways. They introduced the concept of an "inner trigram," a subset of three lines inside a hexagram, and used it in conjunction with the upper and lower trigrams for analysis. It was supposed that each line bore a definite relationship to all other lines in the hexagram, determined by its Yin-Yang nature, its position, and the trigram (upper, lower, or inner) of which it was a part. Thus, a given line "resonated" with this or that line, but "opposed" others. Obviously, the analysis can become so intricate that, whatever the text of the line, one can always find a rationale.

Once the game of line analysis started, the Taoists got into the act by adding a dimension from the "Five Element Theory," a classification of things into the five categories Metal, Wood, Water, Fire, and Earth, which observe a cyclic relationship of "grow" and "kill" (e.g., Earth grows Wood, Water kills Fire). The year and month, as well as day and hour, were supposed to fall successively into one of the five categories. When you start assigning categories to hexagram lines, examining inner hexagrams and whatnot, and add influences due to the time of day, the intricacy becomes staggering, and a whole Taoist astrology grew up around the I Ching.

After the Confucians and the Taoists got through with it, the intrinsic spirit of the I Ching became all but lost in a cloud of pseudo-analysis. Ironically, the original meaning was more apparent to people from other cultures, who were not crippled by "knowing too much." Thus, Wilhelm Leibniz, in eighteenth-century Germany, and Carl Jung, in twentieth-century Switzerland, were both inspired by ideas they perceived in the I Ching that had not impressed the Confucians. We shall now describe what they saw in the I Ching.

There had been an alternative ordering of the hexagrams, the so-called "Fuxi order," which brought to the fore the derivation of the hexagrams from the Yin-Yang concept. One imagines first that Yin and Yang grew out of a primordial Oneness. Next, the Yin and Yang each split into Yin and Yang again and again. The repeated bifurcation eventually produced the sixty-four hexagrams.

We can represent the progression by a tree with two branches issuing from the root. Each branch will give rise to two new branches, and so on. By convention, the left branch will always be Yin. The number of branches in each generation is equal to some power of two (beginning with the zeroth power, which is one). At the sixth generation there are sixty-four branches, which can be identified with the hexagrams. The tree of bifurcations is traditionally depicted in the form of the "segregation diagram."

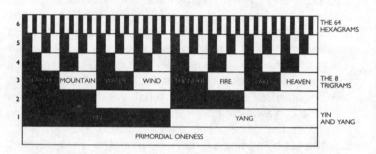

The Fuxi order consists of reading the sixty-four hexagrams from left to right in the highest row of the segregation diagram. The lines making up a hexagram are given immediately below it. For example, the leftmost hexagram (the first one) has six Yin steps below it. The lines are therefore all Yin lines, and make up EARTH. The second one in the sequence has six Yins followed by a Yang, and is therefore LOSS.

As a convenient notation, let us represent Yin by 0 and Yang by 1, so that the symbol for a hexagram can be represented by a string of six digits that are either 0 or 1 that represent the lines in the hexagram when read from left to right. The first few hexagrams in Fuxi order are listed below in this notation:

00000	2 EARTH
00001	23 LOSS
00010	42 SUPPORT
00011	20 VIEW
00100	16 WEARINESS
00101	35 ADVANCE
00110	45 ILLNESS
00111	12 STAGNATION

The list ends with 11110 (43 STRIDE) and 11111 (1 HEAVEN). The ciphers on the left are none other than the integers 0, 1, 2, etc., expressed in binary form.

Leibniz, the mathematician who shares with Newton the credit for the creation of calculus, was thinking about binary integers when he came across the I Ching in 1689. The Jesuit priest Bouvet had sent him a copy from China, with a list of the hexagrams in the Fuxi order and a segregation diagram. Leibniz instantly recognized the hexagram symbols as none other than binary representations of the sixty-four integers from 0 to 63, with EARTH being 0 and HEAVEN 63. He was astounded to find in so ancient a source the very idea he was working on, namely that out of the elementary dyad 0 and 1, one can in principle build everything—the motivation for his study of binary mathematics. In his first full discourse on binary integers, published in 1703, he acknowledged their origin in "the ancient Chinese diagrams of Fohy (Fuxi)." It was his belief that God had revealed the truth to Fuxi three thousand years before his time.

Jung, Swiss psychologist and psychiatrist, founder of analytic psychology, used I Ching consultations as a clinical tool to probe the unconscious. More than that, he took the divination aspect seriously. According to his principle of "synchronicity," the coincidence of events in space and time means something more than mere chance. There is an interdependence of objective events among themselves as well as with the subjective (psychic) states of the observer. Thus, the casting of a hexagram is part of the moment and can be taken as an indicator of the essence of the moment.

COMING FULL CIRCLE

Time has dimmed the authority of the Confucians. The lasting and universal appeal of the I Ching rests in fact not on its role as moral teacher, but as philosopher and oracle. We now perceive the cosmology of Yin and Yang as a powerful allegory instead of physical truth, the latter having been entrusted to science. As explorer of the inner cosmology of human feelings, however, the I Ching is as valid today as it was three thousand years ago. Thus we come full circle in recognizing the I Ching for what it really is: an oracle. The genius that was Zhou created something true to basic human desires and needs, and it has withstood the ravages of history.

5

ROOTS OF THE I CHING

We cannot be sure how much of the traditional story about how the I Ching came to be is believable. It should probably be taken in an allegorical sense, though. Things attributed to one person, such as the trigrams of Fuxi, the hexagrams of King Wen, and the line text of Duke Zhou, were most likely products of a long evolution, rather than the work of any individual. The great sages stand as symbols for ideas that crystallized over time, and the actual way in which the I Ching as we know it came together remains a mystery.

There are, however, significant facts that have come to light very recently, unearthed by scholars digging into

**DIGGING
AMONG RUINS**

the past among ancient ruins and old manuscripts. This archaeological treasure offers material evidence of ancient traditions of divination that were forerunners of the I Ching, and it underscores the I Ching's primary function as an oracle. Interestingly, there are indications that the I Ching was originally one of three Oracles of Change, as is shown in this passage from the Confucian classic, Zhou Li (Zhou Rites), which focuses on the organization of Zhou government:

> The Soothsayer shall be in charge of the three Yi's:
> Lien Shan, Gui Cang, and Zhou Yi.

These vehicles of divination must have evolved over long periods of time, when Zhou was still a vassal state of Shang, and been compiled into standard reference manuals after Zhou received the mantle from Heaven. This is corroborated by the I Ching's obsession with Shang, and the fact that no mention is made of people and events after the time of King Wu, when the Zhou Dynasty was founded. The latest historical references in the I Ching are to Jizi, in 36 THE CRYING PHEASANT, and to Marquis Kang, in 35 ADVANCE.

The recent archaeological findings have also led the way in uncovering many previously historical references in the I Ching, bringing new life and new meaning to stories that had been lost for thousands of years.

THE ORACLE BONES OF SHANG

Just as it seems that the I Ching was one of many oracles at the time, it is also clear that the practice of divination significantly predated the I Ching. The best-known form of ancient divination is preserved in the oracle bones of the Shang Dynasty, uncovered at the turn of the century on the site of An Yang, the last capital of Shang.

These bones (originally tortoise shells and then ox bones when the shell supply ran low) were used by the official soothsayers at the court of Shang, whose charge was to read omens for state matters, such as the weather on the day of a sacrificial ceremony or prospects for a royal hunt. During a divination session, the soothsayer would take a tortoise shell with six depressions made on its back side and apply heat to one of these depressions, causing cracks to appear. He would then read the pattern of cracks on the front side and render judgment. On the very same plate, he would record his name, the date, the question, and the judgment, as well the eventual verification. With six depressions, a tortoise plate was good for six readings.

To inscribe the tortoise shell, the soothsayer would write on it with ink and brush, then incise the characters with a knife and apply black or red paint to bring out the carved characters. The finished product is truly a work of art, bearing individualistic styles of calligraphy. One can discern prevailing calligraphic fashions, which changed over periods of time from Early-Robust to Neo-Delicate. A facsimile of a tortoise plate is shown below. The general pattern of the cracks gave rise to the form of the Chinese character for divination, ｜ .

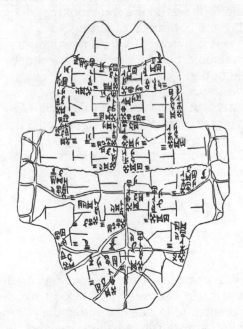

Tortoise shells were not a local product of Shang, but came by tribute from eastern states near the seashore. They were prized items, as the I Ching testifies:

Someone is proffering a tortoise shell
Worth ten double cowries.
It cannot be refused.

(42 INCREASE)

MYSTERY OF THE DRAGON BONES

With the fall of Shang, in 1122 B.C., the tortoise oracle went into oblivion. It was mentioned sporadically in texts from the Zhou era, but no one seemed to know what was actually done. And so the inscribed shells and bones laid buried for three thousand years, under the forgotten ruins of Shang, until chance brought them to light at the turn of our century.

Fragments of oracle bones had been dug up by peasants from time to time and found their way to medicine shops, where they would be ground up and sold as "dragon-bone powder," a cure for all sorts of things. How long this had gone on, no one knows. One day in 1900, the novelist Liu E fell ill and was prescribed "dragon-bone powder." In the medicinal potion brewed from the powder, he found a fragment of incompletely ground "dragon bone," on which ancient scripts could be made out. He bolted straight up from his bed and ran to a friend's house to show him this wonderful discovery. They started an investigation and traced the source of the "dragon bones" to An Yang, the last capital of Shang.

The rest is history. A whole new industry and discipline sprang up around the collecting and deciphering of the oracle bones.

In the 1930s, the Chinese Academy of Science sponsored systematic excavations in An Yang. On the thirteenth expedition, in 1936, the diggers hit a bonanza, the imperial archive of oracle bones. There are reportedly some 100,000 oracle bone fragments extant, in private collections and public museums throughout the world.

PRINCE HAI, MAN OF MYSTERY

Prince Hai's name appeared frequently on the oracle bones, and their discovery has helped to identify the many references to Prince Hai within the I Ching, though his exact importance still remains unclear.

Prior to this new information, his story, as told in Chapter 2, had escaped recognition, not only in the I Ching, but also in various old texts. These include The Book of Mountains and Seas, a collection of ancient fairy tales; The Bamboo Annals, a chronology written on bamboo chits, unearthed in the fourth century in an old tomb, whose account of some historical events was so different from accepted versions that it was branded a forgery; Ask Heaven, a poem by Qu Yuan, possibly the greatest poet of China, who lived in the fourth century B.C. These sources have greater claim to authenticity than most Chinese classics because they were not in the mainstream of Confucian thought and were therefore safe from the rewriters of history.

Until the oracle bones provided the clues, no one really knew what these references meant (though generations of annotators have stated their wrong interpretations with utter confidence and authority). Comparative studies of the old texts finally brought the story to light, after thousands of years.

One wonders, however, why the I Ching mentions Prince Hai so frequently, and with such feeling. Perhaps he was unjustly forced into exile, as suggested by Qu Yuan's angry query in Ask Heaven:

Hai inherited Ji's virtue,
And had his father's trust.
How did he end up in Yi,
To herd sheep and oxen?
. . .

The boy shepherd in Yi
Whence did he encounter?
Hitting the bed to make escape,
What hath fate sent?

We recognize here events mentioned in 56 THE TRAVELER and 23 LOSS. Qu Yuan posed these questions not out of idle curiosity, but in a mood of anger while in exile. The same poem raises generally weighty questions, such as the metaphysical query:

Before the universe took form
How could it be observed?

or a rhetorical one on injustice:

Why did sages of great virtue,
Tempt diverse fate so strange,
That Meikai dismemberment suffered,
And Jizi madness feigned?

Here we recognize the Jizi of 36 THE CRYING PHEASANT.

KING DU DING'S BOAR HUNT

King Wu Ding, the reigning Shang monarch from 1324 to 1235 B.C., was particularly fond of the bone oracle, and the discovery of his archives revealed the ways in which he consulted it. Often he would ask questions about personal matters, such as a toothache. ("Which ancestor have I offended?") The I Ching refers to him in the following passage:

> King Wu Ding warred against Devil's Land,
> And conquered it in three years.
>
> (63 FULFILLMENT)

Top right: End view
Bottom right: Front view
Left: Back view

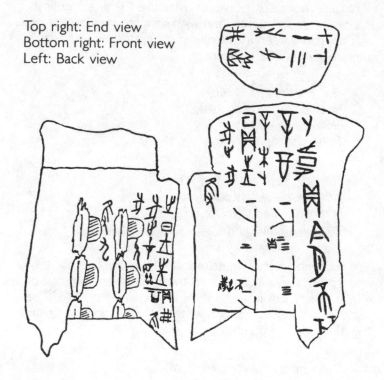

An interesting bone fragment from his archive is shown above. The bone was from the shoulder blade of an ox. In the top view, you can see inscriptions made on the bone edge, which read:

> 1-8. Lady Jing
> delivered three pairs. Yue

This is the procurement record. It says that on the day 1-8, Lady Jing delivered three pairs of shoulder blades and was received by Yue.* From other oracle bones, Lady Jing can be identified as a wife of King Wu Ding. She had a fiefdom of her own and often led armies into battle.

In the front view of the oracle bone, you can see cracks with judgment noted beside them. There were two separate questions asked on this oracle bone. One question started in the first column on the right (reading down):

9-10. Wei divining. This evening will not . . .

Wei was the name of the soothsayer. The question was probably "Will it not rain this evening?" The answer is lost. The other question, which received a favorable answer, starts on the second column:

8-8. Huan divining. To go on boar hunt. Bag?

The back view of the oracle bone shows the depressions for burning. The inscriptions read:

Divining. Bag not?
That day the King hunted boar in Ju.
Indeed, bagged nine.

The first line is an overflow of the question from the front. The question was posed twice: once in the affirmative, once in the negative. The omens were judged to be very auspicious. Thus, when the King got nine boars, the confirmation was recorded with a gleeful "indeed."

A TRUER READING

The oracle bones have also helped lead to a more plausible and faithful interpretation of the I Ching's original language, revealing many instances in which basic oracular pronouncements were mistakenly read as philosophical invocations.

Notice the character for "divine" (zhen), shown be-

---

*Dates were identified by two ordinal characters, the first running from 1 to 10, and the second from 1 to 12; the combination repeats after 60 days. This system is still in use in China, with exactly the same characters.

low in its oracle-bone form on the left and modern form
on the right.

凶　貞

On the oracle bones, this character could have no other
meaning than "to divine" or "divination." However, zhen
has taken on virtuous connotations since the days of
Shang. They include "chastity," "loyalty," and "perseverance"; but "divination" would be designated "now rare" in
an unabridged Chinese dictionary.

Now zhen happens to be a key word in the I Ching.
When one reads it according to its modern meaning, he
finds seemingly strange sayings like "perseverance brings
disaster." But when read according to its oracle-bone
meaning, the mystical irony of "perseverance brings disaster" becomes a mundane "bad omen." Common sense
tells us that this must be what the I Ching really says.

"Perseverance" brings more disaster. The entire hexagram text of Heaven consists of only four characters:

元　　　亨　　　利　　　貞
yuan　　　heng　　　li　　　zhen.

In a word-for-word translation according to modern
meanings, it would read:

Great Well-being Furthering Perseverance.

What on earth does this mean? The Confucians made this
out to be a list of Good Things. The opening of so venerable a book had better contain a venerable message. They
declared them the Four Virtues of the I Ching. The Ten
Wings expounded on the theme with great eloquence.

Now that "perseverance" is recognized as a mislead-
ing literal reading, these words have to be reinterpreted.
A more likely syntax is:

Yuan heng. Li zhen.

Heng (亨) is the archaic form of xiang (享), which
means a sacrificial ceremony. Thus the Four Virtues evap-
orate into something more primitive:

Sign of the Great Sacrifice. Auspicious omen.

It means that the hexagram bears good omen for the
Great Sacrifice, a solemn ritual in which the King makes
offerings to a High Ancestor, or to God.

HOW THE I CHING WAS USED

Interesting vignettes showing the actual use of the I Ching can be found in Zuo Zhuan, historical accounts written by the blind historian Zuo Qiu Ming, contemporary of Confucius. We cite three examples to show the free and individualistic way the I Ching was interpreted by professional soothsayers of the time.

Year 15 of The Duke Xi of Lu (644 B.C.)

When the Earl of Qin launched an attack on the state of Jin, he asked Du Fu the soothsayer to consult the yarrow oracle. A good omen was reported. On the first attack from across the river, the Marquis of Jin retreated.

When pressed about details of the "good omen," Du Fu said: "The situation is very auspicious. You will capture the Marquis after charging him three times. The hexagram was WORK, and the relevant line reads:

Thrice a thousand chariots charge.
After the third wave,
The male fox is captured.

The male fox here clearly refers to the Marquis. The hexagram is Mountain over Wind. Since it's now autumn, and fruits are ripening, it signifies that we shall reap the fruits and take the lumber, while they will lose everything."

The Marquis of Jin suffered three defeats and retreated to Han. On day 9-11, the armies clashed in the field of Han, and the Marquis of Jin was captured and taken to Qin.

Year 16 of The Duke Cheng of Lu (574 B.C.)

When the Marquis of Jin attacked the state of Zheng, the Viscount of Chu came to Zheng's aid. The Chu army arrived at dawn and spread out threateningly to confront the Jin army.

The Marquis of Jin consulted the yarrow oracle and got RETURN, a good omen according to the Keeper of Records. The text reads:

Woe to the south land.
Shoot at its king.
You will hit his eye.

(Chu, a southern state, was eventually defeated.)

Year 9 of The Duke Xiang of Lu (563 B.C.)

The Duchess Mu died in East Palace. Before her death, the yarrow oracle was consulted, and it yielded MOUNTAIN, changing to THE CHASE.

The Keeper of Records told the Duchess, "To chase is to rid. You will soon recover from your illness."

"No," replied the Duchess. "The judgment says 'yuan heng li zhen.' These are the Four Virtues . . . , but I have none of them. I shall die."

In the last example, the hexagram obtained was MOUNTAIN changing to THE CHASE, with five changing lines. Yet the Keeper of Records concentrated on the name of the changed hexagram. This was at variance with usage from other examples in Zuo Chuan, indicating that even then there was no standard way to consult the I Ching, and different states might have had their own systems.

It is interesting that the Duchess disputed the reading of the professional soothsayer and that the Four Virtues were mentioned by name in the last example. The passage we left out in the quote was a verbatim copy of a flowery paragraph in the Ten Wings explaining the Four Virtues—very unlikely utterances from a dying lady. Some late editor must have tampered with the text of Zuo Chuan here.

The hexagram names mentioned above are all familiar ones. However, the texts quoted in the first two cases are nowhere to be found in the present I Ching. Were there different editions of the I Ching used in the different states at the time? Could they have been fragments of the lost Yi's of Zhou? These are fascinating questions to which we have no answers.

ORIGIN OF THE YARROW ORACLE

The ancient Chinese, like ancient peoples elsewhere, were fascinated with integers, especially the so-called "magic squares." It was said that in the time of Fuxi a "dragon horse" emerged from the River (the Yellow River), bearing on its back the "River Diagram." When Yu toured the country in his mission to subjugate the Great Deluge, a striped tortoise came out of the Luo river with the "Luo Tablet" carved on its back. Both are depicted here, with their numerical contents shown below each in modern notation.

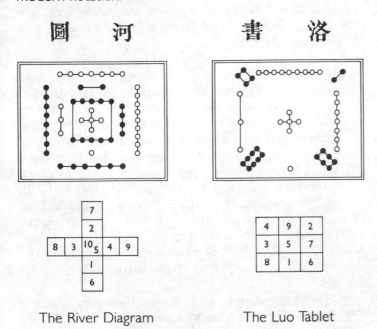

The River Diagram   The Luo Tablet

The "magic" quality of the River Diagram is that the sum of all the odd integers on the periphery, as well as that of the even integers, comes out to be 20: $1+3+7+9 = 2+4+6+8 = 20$. The numbers on the outer layer (6, 7, 8, 9) are those used in the yarrow oracle to designate the four possible values of a line: Old Yin, Young Yang, Young Yin, and Old Yang.

The Luo Tablet has the "magic" property that it uses all the integers, 1 through 9, and that all the integers lying on a line, whether vertical, horizontal, or diagonal, add up to 15. We again recognize the 6, 7, 8, 9 of the yarrow oracle, although their placements in the Luo Tablet do not follow any obvious rule, as in the River Diagram. As we shall see below, however, there is evidence for another form of divination, or a forerunner of the yarrow oracle, in which the numbers used were 1, 2, 5, 6, 7, and 8, which form a contiguous block in the Lo Inscription.

The ancient Chinese used counting sticks (yarrow stalks?) to do arithmetic. The magic squares must have been discovered by playing around with the counting sticks. It is not hard to imagine that divinatory power was ascribed to the outcome of certain manipulations of the sticks. If so, the yarrow oracle, or at least the numerological basis for it, could be older than the bone oracle of Shang or the concept of trigrams and hexagrams. We now have indications from archaeological evidence that this is indeed the case.

As early as the Song Dynasty (twelfth century A.D.), scholars noticed that there were undecipherable "strange characters" on Shang and Zhou bronzes. Similar "strange" inscriptions have been found on oracle bones unearthed in modern times and on earthenware recovered from ancient tombs. There had been various interpretations of these markings, including the suggestion that they were characters from a tribe foreign to either Shang or Zhou.

Everything suddenly fell into place when, in 1978, Zhang Zhenlang proposed at a conference in Changchun, China, that these characters are in fact numerals representing divination lines, like the 6, 7, 8, 9 of the yarrow oracle. This suggestion spurred much interest and research.* A few examples of these markings are reproduced here.

The first example shows inscriptions on an early Zhou cauldron that is a well-known artifact. Only the deciphering is new. It was cast by Keeper of Records Yo, and the inscriptions read:

> *Keeper Yo made this precious vessel.*
> *Divination: 758.*

The "strange characters" are the last three, here read as 758, making up something like a trigram. This is an interesting example, because the Keeper of Records was usually in charge of official divinations.

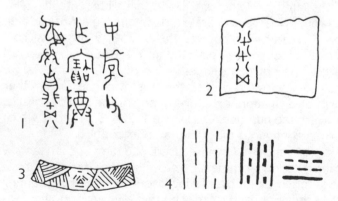

*For a review of recent findings, see the article (in Chinese) by Zhang Yachu and Liu Yu, in *Kaogu (Archaeology)*, 1981, No. 173, pp. 154–163.

From late Shang oracle bones, we have the second example, which shows a series of numerals read as 878785—a hexagram!

Most interesting is the third example, from a pottery urn recovered from a common tomb of the late Shang era in Shantung province. (The piece was reported in *Kaogu*, 1961, No. 2, p. 93.) It bears a hexagram: 188611. The notable fact is that the tomb was that of a common person, in the "eastern barbarian" region far from the seat of Shang power.

Finally we reproduce in the last example markings on late Shang or early Zhou bronze vessels that bear some similarity to the Yin and Yang lines as we know them.

From these preliminary discoveries, we can surmise that divination by numerology was very ancient and widespread and was used even by the common people. It seems plausible that the numerology of the yarrow oracle had its beginning in the magic squares, for regularities in the integers tend to inspire awe. The ideas of Yin, Yang, and change might have been a later creation to put the process on a higher philosophical plane. It might even be true that King Wen formalized the hexagrams, but their existence could have long preceded him.

In human inventions, as exemplified by the creation of a successful theory in physics, the historical route is always tortuous, confused, and illogical. Once the final form has taken shape, however, an "elegant formulation" can be found that makes the whole thing logical, beautiful, and inescapable.

Perhaps the same is true of the I Ching: that the text is a distillation of the divination texts of many generations; that the concepts of Yin, Yang, and change are "elegant formulations" of ideas finalized over centuries.

Perhaps, too, as in physics, the theory that survives is one that "works."

6

I CHING AND PHYSICS

When I was a postdoctoral fellow in physics at the Institute for Advanced Study in Princeton, I worked with Chen Ning Yang on a problem in statistical mechanics. Every morning we would have heated arguments in his office, but rarely, if ever, did we speak about anything other than physics, so concentrated was our interest.

Earlier, Yang had collaborated with Tsung Dao Lee of Columbia University in an attempt to resolve an outstanding puzzle of the time concerning the so-called "weak interactions." In a series of now-classic papers, they had made the bold proposal that nature is not left-right symmetric. Specifically, they suggested that left-right sym-

PERSONAL
REFLECTIONS OF
KERSON HUANG

metry is violated because the neutrino, a spinning sub-atomic particle important for the weak interactions (which also happens to be indispensable in the nuclear process that causes the sun to shine), always "spins to the left," like an advancing left-handed screw.

The proposal led to very specific experimental predictions, and Chien Shiung Wu, an experimental physicist at Columbia, set out to test it with a team at the National Bureau of Standards. After six months of hard work, she and her co-workers verified that left-right symmetry was indeed violated.* The news sent shock waves through the physics community, and Lee and Yang were awarded the Nobel Prize in Physics the following year.

I remember the morning when Yang learned of the news of the downfall of parity. He was excited about the new outlook on physics the discovery brought. Then he said suddenly, "Let's ask the I Ching." We threw the coins in his office and got the hexagram 53 Progress:

> Favorable for a maiden's marriage.
> Auspicious omen.

The body of the hexagram emphasizes that progress comes only gradually.

I think Yang was a little disappointed, but the I Ching has proven to be prophetic. By knocking down a sacred cow, Lee and Yang had led physics across a threshold, beyond which an immense vista opened up. A long fuse was lit, which has been sputtering for thirty years, illuminating vast domains in particle physics and leading to furious attempts to probe matter at a deeper level, even to plumb dimensions beyond space-time. But why the neutrino should be a "left-handed screw" still remains a deep mystery, and perhaps holds the key to further progress.

Strangely enough, the I Ching had never come up in our conversations until that morning. Yet, by the mere fact that we shared a certain Chinese cultural background, it was taken for granted that we both knew about the I Ching. Neither of us believed that the I Ching could predict the future, in the sense that physics predicts the future in certain systems, but there was the unspoken understanding that to consult it was to solemnize the moment.

---

*Precisely because the neutrino is a "left-handed screw," as was recognized shortly after the experiment.

My father, who had a Confucian disdain for fortune-telling and the occult, often consulted the I Ching, an act he looked upon as a kind of homage to tradition. When I left home to come to the U.S. to study, he had cast a hexagram for the occasion and was pleased to have gotten 18 WORK, with the line "taking up the father's work." When I got my Ph.D. in physics, he sent me the "family" I Ching, with that line inscribed on it in his excellent calligraphy.

Cultural heritage tied me to the I Ching in the first place. But among the Chinese classics it had a special and unique fascination for me. I remember reading the first hexagram, I HEAVEN, for the first time as a teenager, and being deeply impressed by the laconic and austere style, the grand symbolism, and the timeless moral.

The idea of constructing a rich allegory of the world from just two basic elements, Yin and Yang, was a revelation that gave me the kind of excitement one can experience only when very young, when the world is a new store of strange, unknown, and wonderful things.

When I found out about theoretical physics somewhat later, I experienced the same kind of excitement, for basically the same reason: Here is something that holds the key to understanding all physical phenomena, starting from postulates of great simplicity and beauty. Yet from the very beginning it was clear to me that physics and the I Ching operate on entirely different levels, although it was hard to say precisely what those levels were.

I went on to choose physics as my profession, but I kept up an interest in the I Ching, avidly following the results of scholarly research on its meaning and origins. I continued to consult the I Ching as oracle, and have found it to be a source of strength and comfort, especially in times of personal crisis and sorrow. Here, however, I offer thoughts on the relationship between physics and the I Ching.

To begin, I should point out some common traps, so we may avoid falling into them.

The "flower children" of the sixties turned to the I Ching, mainly to rebel against what they perceived as the values of a technological society. This is sometimes seen as an indication of the incompatibility between the "spiritual" I Ching and "materialistic" science. That there is no such incompatibility I can personally testify. The beauty of the physical laws is a source of spirituality, and the pursuit of science requires a high degree of idealism. On the other hand, the I Ching, like the Confucianism it helped to engender, is always pragmatic and has its calculating side.

And then there are people, even learned ones, who believe that modern physics, especially quantum physics, has blurred the boundary between the objective world of matter and the subjective world of mind. Such a belief is untenable, arising chiefly from abuse of the technical terms of physics, such as pointing to the "uncertainty principle" as evidence that "uncertainty" has become a part of physics.

Finally, there are those who find it emotionally satisfying to believe that the I Ching anticipated the concepts of modern physics by thousands of years. The truth is, there is no connection between the I Ching's allegorical dynamics of change and the dynamical laws of physics, even in a qualitative sense.

The relationship between what the I Ching represents and what modern physics represents is more elusive and, I believe, has to be sought on a higher plane.

The power of physics is derived first of all from a careful delineation of the boundary between what it can discuss and what it cannot. The motion of water waves is within its domain, but the human emotion evoked by the sight of a breaking tidal wave is not. Within its domain it has succeeded in formulating natural laws of great beauty, which can give quantitative predictions that we can test in laboratory experiments. Outside of its domain of application it keeps an absolute silence.

What characterizes the domain of phenomena that physics can address? The main requirement is that the system under consideration be quantifiable in terms of precisely defined variables that can be measured experimentally. Water waves belong here because they can be completely described in terms of wavelengths, frequencies, amplitudes, and so forth.

An essential element in physics is modeling through idealization. The physicist has to decide what the most relevant variables are for the phenomenon under study and ignore the irrelevant ones. Only then can the system be described by mathematical equations simple enough to be solved. Choosing what to ignore in the idealization is the most important part in the genesis of a theory, the part where intuition and creativity come into play.

Thus, theoretical physics began when Galileo modeled moving bodies by idealized point masses and postulated that only two variables are needed to describe a body's motion: the position and the velocity. When these two quantities are given at a particular time, the future course of the motion is completely determined. This, of course, was the beginning of classical mechanics, which has enabled us to perform miracles like sending a man to the moon.

To decide on an appropriate model, we have to take into account the measuring instruments that will be used on the system. For example, if we are studying the motion of a jellyfish in water, it would not be a good idea to idealize it as a point mass, for its shape affects its motion in an important way. On the other hand, the shape might be irrelevant if we merely want to know how its center moves when it is tossed out of a spaceship into empty space. Physics has been able to get away with drastic idealizations because it deals with simple measuring instruments, such as scales that read between 1 and 10. The wonder is that it works so well.

Everything not in the domain clearly marked out by physics is beyond its grasp, and this is the domain in which the I Ching and other nonscientific endeavors operate. The domain is vast, including such diverse phenomena as the stock market, classical music, and love. In fact, it covers all situations and phenomena in which the "measuring device" is a person.

As time goes on, the domain of physics may expand, taking in new areas that it did not claim before. For example, forecasting the weather used to be an important function of the soothsayer, but it is now the concern of meteorology, which makes use of physical models as much as it can. It makes predictions that may or may not be better than those of the soothsayers, but the basis is sounder, and we can hope to improve the results. Thus, one could argue that perhaps eventually everything will fall into the domain of physics. In fact, the French mathematician Joseph Louis Lagrange (1736-1813) said as much. He pointed out that, given the knowledge of the positions and velocities of every last particle in the universe at a given moment, one can in principle calculate the future course of the universe and, therefore, all the phenomena that will occur in it.

The only trouble with such a vision is that it neglects to take into consideration the measuring instruments for which the output is intended. For example, we can describe a mural by describing every single atom in it. The result might be spat out by a computer as a very long (but finite) sequence of 0's and 1's. This is certainly capable of distinguishing *The Last Supper* from a subway graffito, but it is not useful information because it does not register on the relevant measuring instrument—an art lover. We might think that perhaps someday we will have a computer that can turn that sequence of 0's and 1's into a more usable form, but we don't know how to characterize what is "usable." The only thing that works is for the art lover to look at the mural. Nothing else will do.

For an individual, the ultimate measuring instrument is oneself, which will probably never (heaven forbid) fall into the clutches of physics. Therefore, there is a domain beyond the grasp of physics that can never be reduced to nil, however advanced the science might become. This is where the I Ching enters. For lack of a fancier term, I call it "real life." In real life, no obvious idealizations can be made. How do we know what is relevant and what is not? Maybe everything is relevant, down to the very last detail. Complexity is of the essence. This is perhaps what Jung means by "synchronicity."

To me, then, the I Ching represents a "phenomenological" approach to the extreme complexity of real life, and it is designed to register on the proper measuring instrument—the individual. The ideas of Yin, Yang, and change give us a theory of great simplicity and beauty. The complexity of the situation is modeled by the random element in the casting of a hexagram. The creators of the I Ching might not have described it quite in this manner, but as a physicist in our time, this is how I understand it.

Two developments in the modern era have influenced our views towards the I Ching. First, the advent of modern psychology has made the interpretation of symbols and images of the I Ching a more familiar and acceptable process for self-understanding and decision-making.

Secondly, in the sphere of intellectual thought, we have moved away from the rigidly mechanistic world view of the nineteenth century. We have come to appreciate the fact that the world is truly complex, that there will always be "random" elements we cannot pin down, even if the underlying laws are known.

I do not profess to understand "synchronicity," and I do not believe that the I Ching can foresee the future in an objective sense. I take the pragmatic approach that the function of an oracle is to satisfy certain needs of the person seeking counsel (including the need to know the future). In this sense I have found that the I Ching works.

7

USING THE
I CHING

To use the I Ching for divination, you "cast a hexagram" by
picking out the six lines according to definite rules, which
we shall describe later. Each of the lines you choose can
be one of four possibilities, corresponding to either Yin
or Yang, and either changing or unchanging. The six
chosen lines give you an "original hexagram," symbolizing
an initial situation, and a "changed hexagram," corresponding to the eventual development.

    The dynamics of change expand the sixty-four static
hexagrams into more than four thousand patterns of development. Since there are sixty-four possible original
hexagrams, and each one can change into one of sixty-

**I CHING
AS ORACLE**

four final hexagrams, the number of possible combinations is $64 \times 64 = 4{,}096$.

When you consult the I Ching, then, you can get over four thousand different readouts. Of course, no two people would interpret a message the same way, nor would the same person interpret a message the same way on different occasions. Hence the real possibilities are limited only by your imagination.

The original method for casting a hexagram consists of manipulating forty-nine straws of yarrow, a reed with straight, stiff stalks. This is know as the "yarrow oracle." Since the process is intricate and time-consuming, an alternative "coin oracle" was devised, in which you toss coins to generate the lines of a hexagram. However, the two methods are not equivalent, for they give different probabilities for the lines.

THE COIN ORACLE

Take three coins and toss them. There are four possible outcomes: three heads, two heads, two tails, and three tails. Each of these can be associated with a hexagram line, according to the rules given in the accompanying table.

Combination	Symbol	Line	Probability
3 tails		Old Yang (changing to Yin)	1/8
2 heads		Young Yang (unchanging)	3/8
2 tails		Young Yin (unchanging)	3/8
3 heads		Old Yin (changing to Yang)	1/8

To cast a hexagram, you have to throw the coins six times in succession. After the first throw, you draw the symbol for the line on a piece of paper. This is line 1. After the second throw, you draw the symbol for the new line above the first one, and call it line 2. The process is repeated until all six lines are obtained.

In the yarrow oracle described below, Old Yang is associated with the number 9 and Old Yin with 6. For this reason, the I Ching associates a Yang line with 9, and a Yin line with 6. Thus, for example, the fifth Yin line of a hexagram is labeled 6-5, sometimes translated as "six in the fifth place."

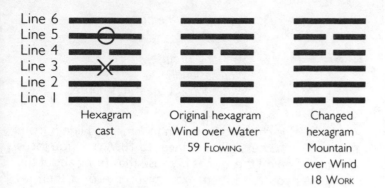

Line 6
Line 5
Line 4
Line 3
Line 2
Line 1

Hexagram
cast

Original hexagram
Wind over Water
59 FLOWING

Changed
hexagram
Mountain
over Wind
18 WORK

GETTING THE HEXAGRAM

You now have a stack of six lines, as illustrated in the figure. They naturally give rise to an "original hexagram" and a "changed hexagram." As the name implies, the "original hexagram" is gotten by accepting the lines as Yin or Yang regardless of whether they are young or old. The "changed hexagram" is obtained from the original one by changing the old lines to their opposites.

To find the names of the hexagrams you have obtained, divide each hexagram into an upper and lower trigram and look up the number of the hexagram in the matrix of hexagram numbers given in the Appendix.

In the example illustrated, the original hexagram is Wind over Water. You go to column 6 (Wind) of the matrix in the Appendix and read down to row 4 (Water), where you find the entry 59. This tells you that the hexagram Wind over Water is hexagram 59. You can easily locate that in the text: 59 FLOWING. Similarly, the changed hexagram is Mountain over Wind, which gives 18 WORK.

Sometimes you can get a hexagram with no changing lines. In that case the hexagram has an unchanging identity, connoting a static situation.

READING THE MESSAGE

Having cast the hexagram and found the original and the changed forms, you then read the changing lines in the original hexagram. In our illustration they are as follows:

▄▄ ▄▄ **3** *Water laves the body.*
No regrets.

▄▄▄▄▄ **5** *Sweating profusely,*
Wailing loudly.
Water laps at the King's house.
It's safe.

When line 3 is changed from Yin to Yang, and line 5 from Yang to Yin, the hexagram changes to 18 WORK. You focus your attention on these lines because they bring about the change. As you read them, you might interpret them as follows: "Water washes over my body, and it is a good feeling. But wait, a lot of sweating and howling is going on. A flood is coming up to some VIP's house. But it is safe."

Then again, you might have quite different reactions. What the lines mean depends on your associations, and there is no "standard" meaning. The original intention of whoever wrote it three thousand years ago, if there ever was an intention, has long been lost.

You could think about the symbolism of the original hexagram and that of the changed one. The original hexagram, FLOWING, is composed of Wind over Water, while the changed hexagram, WORK, is Mountain over Wind.
You might say that the original situation was fluid, like water driven by wind. Danger lurks in this situation, as implied by the key lines; but safety is assured if one works to secure it, much like making a barrier to block the wind.

The "hexagram text," the reading associated with the hexagram as a whole, and called "the judgment" by Richard Wilhelm in his translation, sets the general context for the specific reading. A look at the new hexagram that is formed by the changing lines also helps to inform the general direction of the reading.

Our commentaries to these hexagrams will help you interpret their meaning by discussing the general theme and the historical references contained in the hexagrams. Understanding that there is a historical background to FLOWING (in that the Shang Dynasty, the one preceding that of the I Ching, moved its capital frequently because of devastation by floods) helps to clarify the meaning of the imagery in the lines. The hexagram WORK, as the commentary there points out, dwells on the conflicts that arise in following parental footsteps.

You can play with all these ideas and elaborate on them endlessly. A quick reading consists of just reacting instinctively to the changing lines.

- If there are no changing lines, read the hexagram text.
- If some lines change, but not all, read the changing lines.
- If all six lines are changing, the situation calls for special treatment. In the case of Heaven changing to Earth, or vice versa, read the dynamic lines provided. For all other hexagrams undergoing total change, read the hexagram text of the changed hexagram.

GENERAL RULES

You must start with fifty yarrow stalks. (Bamboo skewers or drinking straws might be used as substitutes for yarrow stalks.) Set one aside unused.

THE YARROW ORACLE

To cast one line of a hexagram, you need to make three "Changes." A Change is effected through the following steps:

1. Start with 49 yarrow stalks. (We shall loop back to this step later with fewer than 49 stalks. For flexibility, denote the number of stalks by N, with $N = 49$ initially.)

2. Divide the N stalks into 2 piles at random (with at least two in each pile).

3. Take one from the left pile and set it aside.

4. Count off the left pile of stalks in groups of 4. Set aside the remainder, which is either 1, 2, 3, or 4.

5. Repeat step 4 for the right pile (without setting one aside beforehand).

6. Collect all the stalks from both piles that have *not* been set aside.

The above constitutes a Change. The first Change is labeled Change 1. The number of stalks collected after Change 1 has the possible values

$$N(1) = 44, 40$$

with relative probabilities 3:1.

To effect Change 2, go to step 1 above, using $N(1)$ in place of N. The number of stalks collected after Change 2 has the possible values

$$N(2) = 40, 36, 32$$

with relative probabilities 6:8:2.

For Change 3, go to step 1 above, using $N(2)$ in place of N. The number of stalks collected after Change 3 has the possible values

$$N(3) = 36, 32, 28, 24$$

and the relative probabilities stand in the ratios 12:28:20:4.

A line is now cast. You divide N(3) by 4 to obtain the "intrinsic number" of the line. The possible outcomes are listed in the accompanying table.

Intrinsic Number	Symbol	Line	Probability
9	═══○═══	Old Yang (changing to Yin)	3/16
8	══ ══	Young Yin (unchanging)	7/16
7	═══════	Young Yang (unchanging)	5/16
6	═══✕═══	Old Yin (changing to Yang)	1/16

To get another line, go back to step 1 with N set to 49, and start all over again. Since three Changes are required to get a line, casting a hexagram calls for eighteen Changes in all. The process is conducive to contemplation and will generally take fifteen minutes to half an hour. Some prefer the yarrow oracle for this very reason.

FROM THE TEN WINGS

The numerology of the yarrow oracle probably had very ancient roots in the "magic squares" described in Chapter 5. But the earliest explanation we have of its basis comes from one of the Ten Wings. We shall append it here for reference. The parenthetical remarks indicate operations to be performed on the yarrow stalks:

• The number of the Great Change is 50, of which 49 are functional. (Take 50 yarrow stalks, but use only 49.)
• Halve them to symbolize the Two. (Divide the stalks into 2 piles.)
• Set aside one to make the Three. (Set one aside from a pile.)
• Group into fours to represent the Seasons. (Count off the stalks in the pile in groups of four.)
• Put the remainder between fingers to symbolize incommensurability. (Set aside the remainder.)
• Every five years this becomes manifest through leap months. Therefore, repeat the procedure, and then collect the round-offs. (Repeat the procedure for the other pile, and then collect all stalks not set aside, from both piles.)

The coin oracle became more popular than the yarrow oracle because it is more convenient to use; but it gives different probabilities for the lines and might be viewed as less "authentic." Lest you think the yarrow oracle sacrosanct, however, it should be noted that it was once considered inferior to an older form of divination, the tortoise oracle, which consists of reading the cracks produced in tortoise shells by a ritual application of heat.

The tortoise oracle was the court oracle of the Shang Dynasty. Its successor, the Zhou Dynasty, opted for the more convenient and economical yarrow. However, the tortoise oracle continued to be used in early Zhou times, especially for important questions, as an additional assurance. It is reported in the Book of Records that Duke Zhou consulted the oracles about a serious illness incurred by King Wu, his brother and founder of the dynasty:

> Three tortoises were used.
> All gave good omens.
> The chest was then opened, and the Book read.
> It also gave a good omen.

The "Book" probably refers to the I Ching, or a forerunner thereof. In the I Ching itself, there is reference to the possibility that different oracles give conflicting omens:

> Straight and square.
> Though omens be inconsistent,
> No obstacles encountered.
>   (2 EARTH)

As late as some seven centuries after the creation of the I Ching, in the Era of Spring and Autumn, there were purists who still considered the yarrow a poor substitute for the tortoise. One of these traditionalists was quoted in Zuo Chuan (a history book contemporary with Herodotus of ancient Greece) as saying, "The yarrow is short, the tortoise long."

But the increasing complexity of daily life, with its premium on convenience and efficiency, favored the yarrow over the tortoise. In the same way, the coin oracle has become more popular than the yarrow oracle, not only because it is quicker, but because coins are more likely to be found in households than yarrow stalks.

There are probably hundreds of variations on this method of using the I Ching. A popular variation for many

THE DIFFERENT ORACLES

people is found in Chinese temples. It makes use of a number of bamboo strips placed in an open-topped container. On the bamboo strips are written judgments, which could be lines from the I Ching but more often are simpler and clearer messages. The seeker reverently and gently shakes the container until one of the strips falls out. The message is then read.

There is a prevalent form of hexagram consultation that dispenses with the text of the I Ching altogether and reads the omen purely from the Yin-Yang structure of the hexagram and its conjunction with the composition of the day and month according to the "Five Element Theory." Here one goes off on a tangent to a form of Taoist astrology.

A prominent Chinese banker in Singapore who emigrated from Vietnam during the sixties learned from his father an "infallible" way to get answers from the I Ching: The names of the sixty-four hexagrams are written on a piece of paper, arranged in a circular ring. He dangles a ball bearing attached to a gold chain over the piece of paper, concentrating very hard on a question in the meantime. The ball bearing will stop at the hexagram that gives the answer, and, according to him, the result is reproducible if he asks the same question.

People living in California, who spend all their lives driving on freeways, reputedly generate hexagrams by noting the license numbers of passing cars. But this works only for "Ching freaks," who know the I Ching by heart.

And the inevitable happens. You can now consult the I Ching on your personal computer, which will not only cast your hexagram, but print out the relevant lines on the computer screen or the printer. This facility is provided by a software disk that is a companion to this book. You press a key at the right moment, and the software program generates the hexagram according to the yarrow oracle (with the help of the random number generator in the computer). This should be a particularly felicitous way to invoke the Oracle, for the computer naturally thinks in terms of Yin and Yang, which the computer engineer calls 0 and 1.

Let no one say, "The disk is short, the yarrow long."

THE HEXAGRAMS

HEAVEN

OVER

HEAVEN

1 HEAVEN

Sign of the Great Sacrifice.
Auspicious omen.

1 The dragon is hibernating.
Do not act.

2 The dragon is seen in the fields.
Auspicious to see the great personage.

3 A gentleman works hard all day,
And keeps alert in the evening.
In peril, safe.

4 The dragon is sometimes leaping in the pool.
Safe and sound.

5 The dragon is flying in the sky.
Auspicious to see the great personage.

6 The dragon is stranded in the shallows.
Regrets come.

DYNAMIC LINE

A group of dragons is seen without heads.
Good omen.

COMMENTARY

Pure Yang, HEAVEN embodies all that is strong, creative, forward moving. Its symbol is the dragon, that powerful and lofty dweller of the clouds, visible only to the chosen. Traditionally the dragon represents the force of goodness and was the symbol of the Son of Heaven, the Emperor. In this hexagram we follow the development of a powerful idea or personality through the metaphor of the dragon. It makes its tentative debut in the world, flexes its muscles, and achieves supreme success. However, success can breed arrogance and carelessness, and lead to eventual downfall.

THE JUDGMENT

This hexagram is a good omen for an important occasion of state, an imperial sacrificial rite.

THE LINES

1 This is a time of preparation. A challenge is taking shape.

2 Emerging from obscurity, the dragon comes out into the open. Good omen for seeking counsel from someone you respect.

3 Attend to the task at hand and be on guard.

4 In flexing your muscles, you feel your own power.

5 Triumph brings a feeling of exultation, but it is still wise to consult someone you respect.

6 Overconfidence will lead to misadventure and regret.

DYNAMIC LINE

Only HEAVEN and EARTH have a dynamic line, the one to be read when all six lines change. In this case, pure Yang changes to pure Yin! A group of dragons disappears into the clouds, signifying the total retirement of all that is strong and assertive. The regime of the pure Yin will begin.

EARTH

OVER

EARTH

2 EARTH

Sign of the Great Sacrifice.
Auspicious for the mare.
The gentleman goes somewhere.
He gets lost at first,
But finally finds a patron.
All goes well.
It is favorable to go southwest,
Where a friend will be found.
To the northeast, a friend will be lost.
Omen of peace.

1 Treading on frost.
Hard ice cometh.

2 Straight and square.
Though omens be inconsistent,*
No obstacles encountered.

3 Shang is vanquished.
Some things are possible.
Should you serve the King,
There would be no achievement,
But a good ending.

4 A closed bag.
No blame, no praise.

5 A yellow robe.**
Great auspicious omen.

6 The dragons fight in the field.
Their blood runs black and yellow.***

DYNAMIC LINE

Everlasting well-being.

*In the time of Shang and early Zhou, both the Yarrow Oracle and the Bone Oracle were consulted on important questions, and they often gave conflicting advice.
**Symbol of office.
***Black is the color of heaven and yellow that of earth.

COMMENTARY

Pure Yin, EARTH embodies all that is nurturing, receptive, forgiving. Yin is reticent and complicated, in contrast to the clarity and brightness of Yang. Overall, pure Yin is the sign of peace.

THE JUDGMENT

In an agricultural society, questions relating to the breeding of mares and gelding of stallions were often asked of the Oracle. The mare is favored in this hexagram because Earth is all female. As for the male, timing and place are of the essence. Some are auspicious and some not.

THE LINES

1 Pay attention to small warnings; hard times lie ahead.

2 The signs may point to contrary things, but there is only one proper way to act: Be straight and fair in your dealings.

3 Even the seemingly impossible can be achieved: Witness how the Zhou vanquished the evil empire Shang.

4 The issue is settled. You do not gain, but neither will you lose.

5 You will receive an honor.

6 The force of Yin has reached its peak and must give way to Yang, but not without a ritualistic battle.

DYNAMIC LINE

Pure Yin is changing to pure Yang! There is a complete turnaround of the situation, and a rejuvenation is expected. True to form, pure Yin relinquishes power graciously, with a benediction.

WATER

OVER

THUNDER

3 RETRENCHMENT

Sign of the Great Sacrifice.
Auspicious omen.
Do not go anywhere.
Appoint helpers.

1 Build fences.
Settle down.
Appoint helpers.

2 Hustle-bustle,
Carriages and horses ashuffle.
They're not robbers, only wife grabbers.*
The maiden's marriage is not in the signs.
In ten years she shall marry.

3 Hunting deer without a guide,
One merely gets lost in the woods.
The wise would give up.
Going meets with obstacles.

4 Carriages and horses ashuffle.
If you seek marriage, go.
Nothing stands in the way.

5 Saving the fat.
Good omen for small things,
Bad for big things.

6 Carriages and horses ashuffle.
Tears flow plentifully.

*This alludes to a marriage custom in which the groom's party feigns an abduction of the bride, as testimonial to the bride's desirability.

COMMENTARY

In times of difficulty, getting sound advice from competent people is important for success. Other factors are necessary as well: careful preparation, timing, and the ability to distinguish reality from illusion.

Seeking a mate is used as a metaphor to illustrate these points. You need go-betweens. You should know how to make an impression, and you cannot rush things.

THE JUDGMENT

It is not a propitious time to advance; you need to wait and to get help.

THE LINES

1 Strengthen your base of operations with strong defenses and good helpers.

2 All the sound and fury are staged. Conditions are not yet ripe and will not be for some time to come.

3 Without guidance from someone who knows the terrain, you will simply get lost. You might as well give up and save yourself some trouble.

4 It is time to act, but only after preparations have been made.

5 Saving scraps helps only in small things. For big things you have to have a larger vision.

6 Forcing things prematurely brings regret.

MOUNTAIN

OVER

WATER

4 BLINDNESS

Sign of the Sacrifice.
It was not I who sought the novice.
The novice sought me.
The first time you asked, I answered.
Asking three times is impertinent,
And I will not respond.
Good omen.

1 The cataract is clearing.
Good omen for one condemned.
The shackles may be off,
But walking is difficult.

2 The cook is blind.
Auspicious for taking a daughter-in-law.
The son will have a family.

3 Do not marry the girl.
She sees the gold and not the man.
Nothing good will come of it.

4 Trapped and blinded.
Difficulty.

5 Childlike naiveté.
All goes well.

6 Strike the blind only in defense,
Never in offense.

COMMENTARY

The Chinese character translated here as blindness has other connotations as well. It conveys a quality of childish unawareness or innocence, a state of being educable but not yet educated. The message admonishes us to be patient and trusting in our learning. We must proceed in a step-by-step manner, always having faith in the guidance offered by the Oracle.

THE JUDGMENT

Inexperience can make you blind to many things. Although it is important to seek advice from experts, persistent questioning can make you a pest.

THE LINES

1 Obstacles are beginning to recede. You are being freed from the prison of ignorance. Some difficulties remain though, and you will not be able to function smoothly just yet.

2 It may be necessary to have some assistance in performing regular duties. Getting this help will enable the family to prosper.

3 The person you are involved with is shallow and untrustworthy; do not allow the relationship to develop any further.

4 Not paying attention can lead you into a trap. Beware.

5 Not paying attention to your surroundings can sometimes be charming in its innocence.

6 Sometimes it may be necessary to strike out in self-defense, but aggressive action against the unprotected is not acceptable.

WATER

OVER

HEAVEN

5 WAITING

The penalty is a goblet of wine.*
Sign of the Sacrifice.
Good omen.
Auspicious for crossing the great stream.

1 Waiting on the outskirts.
You should be patient.
No troubles.

2 Waiting in the sand.
There is a small altercation,
But all ends well.

3 Waiting in the mud.
Robbers are enticed to come.

4 Waiting in the nave,
Emerging from the cave.

5 Refraining from food and drink.
Good omen.

6 Entering the cave.
Three uninvited guests arrive.
If you treat them with respect,
All will end well.

*To dispose of offerings left over from a sacrificial ceremony, party games were played in which the loser had to drink.

COMMENTARY

The Oracle teaches us to be patient. What is now yields inevitably to what will be; all things are passing, and nothing is unchanging. Perception of the flow of Yin and Yang enables us to wait without anxiety. Free from hope or expectation, doubt, confusion, and frustration, we can await the coming of both good fortune and peril with equanimity. Courage comes from inner security and is expressed in resolute action and perseverance. Preparation of the body and mind during a period of waiting allows us to face the most terrifying events with cool, deliberate resolve.

THE JUDGMENT

The people blocking your way are just playing out a game. The waiting is over. This is a good time to act and move forward.

THE LINES

1 You are still somewhat removed from the problem at hand. Be patient and all will be well.

2 Taking a stand on shifting ground will lead to minor problems, which can be resolved eventually.

3 Allowing yourself to become mired in doubt weakens your position and makes you vulnerable to attack.

4 Doubts have given way to despair, but it will be overcome, and you will see the light again.

5 Occasionally it is helpful to refrain from common pleasures. Fasting frees both the mind and the body.

6 Confronting your deepest fears brings support from an unexpected source. If you are gracious and open to help, problems can be resolved, however difficult they may seem.

HEAVEN

OVER

WATER

6 THE COURT

The punishment is postponed.
But be alert.
Luck ends in misfortune.
Auspicious to see the great personage.
Not auspicious to cross the great stream.

1　Leaving one's work unfinished
Draws a small reprimand.
But all will end well.

2　Having lost in court,
He returned and fled.
The three hundred households of his town
Were thus spared harm.

3　The store of goodwill is eroded.
Danger, but all ends well.
Should you serve the King,
Nothing would be achieved.

4　Having lost in court,
He returned to follow rules,
Accepting defeat.
Good omen for settling down.

5　Great success in court.

6　A belt of honor is bestowed, perhaps,
And recalled thrice in one morning.

COMMENTARY

Apparently this hexagram preserves fragments of a folk-tale or historical episode that has otherwise been lost. The story concerns a certain nobleman who was charged with misconduct at the King's court.

This can prove to be a deeply disturbing hexagram, for it vividly underscores the capriciousness of fate. In the midst of honor comes humiliation; good fortune is ephemeral. No matter how arduously a goal is pursued, the prize could easily slip away. We are exposed to both the light and the dark sides of life. And this we know truly: The tide always turns.

THE JUDGMENT

This is a good time to seek sound advice and counsel, but it is not a time to undertake any major projects or make any significant decisions. You have narrowly escaped some deserved punishment, but you are not yet free of danger. Bide your time and be careful.

THE LINES

1 The problem began when his work was not done on time. This led to a rebuke, but nothing serious.

2 The punishment escalated: He was hauled into court and found guilty. He returned to his power base and then fled. He did not have a chance to take it out on the people under him.

3 There was nowhere to flee. Both the people and the King lost faith in him. He redeemed the situation by realizing this.

4 Accepting defeat and repenting, he became at peace with himself.

5 He was vindicated at court, thus regaining his reputation.

6 You cannot afford to be smug in success. The King giveth, and the King taketh away.

EARTH

OVER

WATER

7 THE ARMY

Auspicious for the great personage.
No troubles.

1   A marching army must have discipline.
Otherwise disaster will befall it,
Even if it has strength.

2   Flourishing in the ranks.
Safe and sound.
The King thrice bestows titles.

3   The army might be carrying corpses.
Misfortune.

4   The army camps on the left.
Safe and sound.

5   Bagging game in a hunt.
Favorable omen for catching an escapee.
No troubles.
The elder son commands the army.
The younger brother hauls corpses.
Omen of misfortune.

6   The King bestows titles.
To found a state, head a clan,
Use not common people.

COMMENTARY

The army was the instrument by which the Zhou seized power from the Shang, as was the case when the Shang had seized power from the Xia, almost a millennium before the I Ching. In both cases, the victor merely carried out the mandate of Heaven, or so it claimed. But without an army, the most righteous cause could not have prevailed. It is therefore natural that we find reference to the army in the I Ching, the oracle of the newly victorious Zhou. We follow the perils and rewards of a commander and are apprised of the importance of choosing good leadership based on merit.

THE JUDGMENT

This hexagram bodes well particularly for a person in a leadership position.

THE LINES

1 Strength without discipline will lead not to victory but defeat.

2 There are rewards for performing well in the ranks; honors, land, and wealth from the King.

3 Being in the ranks carried perils: death in battle.

4 Taking a defensive position for a breather.

5 There are successes and failures in battle: taking prisoners in victory, suffering losses in defeat. Leadership chosen not by merit but by nepotism can lead to defeat.

6 The founding of the Zhou state relied on a coterie of able advisors, among them Duke Zhou (who was credited with compiling the I Ching), and Chief-of-Staff Lu Wan, who emerged from obscurity and retirement to lead the army. There is a natural aristocracy of talent, and leadership must be reserved for the uncommon few of rare abilities.

WATER

OVER

EARTH

8 SUPPORT

Good fortune.
Original oracle: "Eternal well-being."*
The rebellious cometh.
Last to arrive, he meets his end.**

1   When punishments are due,
It is blameless to lend counsel.
The penalty is a jugful of wine.***
In the end, troubles.
But good will come of it.

2   Supporting from within.
Good omen.

3   Supporting an evil person.
Misfortune.

4   Supporting from without.
Good omen.

5   Deed of a famed counselor:
The King lost the game after three chases,
But the townsfolk were spared his wrath.
Good omen.

6   Giving counsel, losing one's head.
Misfortune.

*This line most likely includes the comment of an editor, accidentally retained as part of the text.
**This refers to a story of Emperor Yu, founder of the Xia Dynasty (the one preceding the Shang, which preceded the Zhou), who executed a particularly insubordinate vassal on the pretext of his late arrival at a meeting. (See Chapter 2.)
***This refers to a penalty drink at a party game. See note in hexagram 5.

COMMENTARY

Support here means to help and to complement, as in the support an imperial advisor gives to the King as ruler of the people. History confers special honors to those who say what is right rather than what the King wants to hear.

The present hexagram shrewdly assesses the pitfalls and advantages of serving the powerful and mighty. Support can be given in many forms, but when it is given as advice, it must be judicious and prudent. An inner source of strength is necessary for effectiveness and self-preservation.

This hexagram complements 39 ADMONISHMENT, which deals with the giving of advice in particular.

THE JUDGMENT

The story of Emperor Yu executing the defiant Fang Feng is used to illustrate the importance of using the proper strategy to carry out a plan. In this case the strategy was undoubtedly devised by Yu's advisors.

THE LINES

1 You can counsel a guilty party in good conscience. You might get a slap on the wrist, but you will feel good about discharging your duty.

2 Self-confidence based on inner strength and self-knowledge portends success.

3 Be careful to whom you give your support.

4 Support could be given in the form of external assistance.

5 This appears to be a fragment from a long-lost tale recounting the helpful act of a famed imperial advisor who, through his tact and discretion, managed to prevent a frustrated king from venting his wrath on some innocent townsfolk.

6 When advice displeases, the advisor is at personal risk.

WIND

OVER

HEAVEN

9 SMALL CATTLE

Sign of the Sacrifice.
Thick clouds and no rain,
From my west field cometh.

	1	Reverting to my own ways. Who can blame me? All's well.
	2	Being led home. Good omen.
	3	The wheel comes off the cart. Husband and wife quarrel.
	4	The punishment draws blood. Go, exit gingerly, and be safe.
	5	The punishment is prison For enriching oneself at a neighbor's expense.
	6	It rained, and it cleared. A carriage picks you up. Danger for a woman. After the full moon, Misfortune for a gentleman.

COMMENTARY

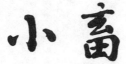

Small cattle symbolize a small farm, a new household, a person's new career. There is an unusual amount of conflict depicted in the lines: breakdowns, quarrels, punishment, and misfortune. On the other hand, there is opportunity to further oneself by maintaining one's integrity and deepest values.

THE JUDGMENT

The image of heavy clouds promising rain that has not yet arrived conveys a mood of expectation and anxiety. There is a sense of impending storm.

THE LINES

1 Maintaining your integrity carries no guilt and is always the best position to take in any quandary.

2 You are in touch with most deeply felt values.

3 Things fall apart. Domestic crises arise.

4 Physical violence breaks out. You should withdraw.

5 Exploiting others will bring severe punishment.

6 Tensions are released and opportunity calls. Don't get carried away.

HEAVEN

OVER

LAKE

10 TREADING

Treading on the tiger's tail: It bites not.
Sign of the Sacrifice.

1 Go safely, in shoes unadorned.

2 A walkway broad and level.
   Good omen for a prisoner.

3 The blind can see.
   The lame can walk.
   Treading on the tiger's tail: It bites.
   Misfortune.
   A military man becomes king.

4 Treading on the tiger's tail: Fearful situation.
   All ends well.

5 A broken shoe.
   Danger.

6 Watch your steps
   Up to the temple of learning.
   The return will be glorious.

COMMENTARY

The Chinese character for the name of this hexagram means "shoe," and hence, "step," "walk," and "treading." The character takes on these various meanings in different lines of the hexagram. The hexagram is about taking steps as a means of getting somewhere, both in a literal and symbolic sense. You have to pay attention to the footgear, what you might step on, and most importantly, the direction you are taking.

THE JUDGMENT   Taking a risky step pays off. It is time to be thankful.

THE LINES

1   Plain dealing will keep you out of trouble.

2   An escape route is open.

3   You have done the impossible. Flush with success, you took a careless step and got hurt. Amidst the confusion a strong man takes over.

4   You can be safe on dangerous ground if you are mindful of your step.

5   It is not possible to go places without the wherewithal.

6   Direct your steps towards learning. The rewards will be great.

EARTH

OVER

HEAVEN

11 PEACE

Small loss, big gain.
All's well.
Sign of the Sacrifice.

1 Plucking reeds to feed the horse,
Using only the stems.
Auspicious to advance.

2 Fording the river with a hollowed gourd,
Taking your friends along.
Regret disappears.
Rewards come in mid-journey.

3 No plains are without bumps.
Whatever goes must return.
Hardship is in store, but no harm will come.
Don't mind the penalty.
Take the wine with your food.*

4 A dandy man lost a fortune
On account of his neighbor:
The price of unwariness.

5 Emperor Yi betrothed his daughter,**
With her niece as consort.***
Great auspiciousness.

6 The wall topples into the moat.
Hold the army.
The town sounds alarm.
Omen of jeopardy.

*See note in hexagram 5 WAITING.
**Emperor Yi of Shang gave his daughter in marriage to King Wen. (See Chapter 2.) The event forms the theme of 54 THE MARRYING MAIDEN.
***When a noble woman was married off, a female companion went along to the new household as a second consort.

COMMENTARY

A strategy for peace is outlined, against the historical backdrop of the conflict between the Shang people, who held power, and the emerging Zhou people (creators of the I Ching) who were seeking it. We are warned against overconfidence and instructed in maximizing our defenses so as to live in peace with a powerful neighbor. Keeping peace requires that we act appropriately, maintain close relationships with friends, expect hardship as part of the price of living, and take pleasure when and where it is appropriate.

THE JUDGMENT

Some small sacrifices may be called for in order to attain your larger goal. Generally favorable.

THE LINES

1 Take good care of the instruments you need to realize your goal.

2 Even under perilous circumstances, do not leave friends behind. You may need them later, and taking them along gives you the benefit of their presence and support.

3 You cannot expect your path to run smoothly ahead at all times. Life brings occasional hardships; there are always obstacles to overcome. You may meet with setbacks, but your success is assured. It is best not to dwell on these problems but continue to enjoy the good in life as you struggle to overcome the bad.

4 Your carelessness and misjudgment can easily lead to your downfall. Be very careful of whom you trust, particularly where finances are involved.

5 Good fortune, particularly with regard to relationships.

6 Do not take advantage of your enemy's crumbling defenses. Seeming disarray may be a trap.

HEAVEN

OVER

EARTH

12 OBSTRUCTION

Evil people clog the way.
It bodes ill for the good.
Big loss, small gain.

1　Plucking reeds to feed the horse,
Using only the stems.
Good omen.
Sign of the Sacrifice.

2　The ceremonial meat is wrapped in palm.
Good omen for common people,
Bad for the gentleman.*
Sign of the Sacrifice.

3　The cooked meat is wrapped in palm.

4　A title comes.
Troubles go.
Longevity and fortune to follow.

5　A fear of obstruction.
Good omen for the great personage.
Treachery! Treachery!
Hang on to the mulberry.

6　Temporary obstruction
Followed by jubilation.

*According to rituals, ceremonial meat should be offered in a proper bronze vessel.

COMMENTARY

There is frequently a gap between our hopes and expectations and our current reality. Such dissonance can create either frustration, fury, despair, or keen ambition and drive, depending upon our response. Caught between the desire to move and a stagnant environment, we can draw strength from our basic values to overcome the obstacles. Making the proper offerings (prayer, meditation, good works, ritual observances) can result in honors, wealth, and a long and fruitful life, according to the Oracle.

THE JUDGMENT

Your path is obstructed by difficulties created by untrustworthy people.

THE LINES

1 Using only the correct materials and instruments will enable you to accomplish your task.

2 Different things are required of different people, depending upon their levels of development. More is expected of the advanced, so they must be careful to be sincere in their works.

3 Palm-wrapping of meat is inappropriate for formal occasions, but as a cooking technique it is excellent for everyday meals.

4 Honors, wealth, health, and a long life are in store as problems disappear.

5 Mulberry leaves are fed to silkworms. The cultivation of silkworms was traditionally one of the basic home industries in China. Keeping close to traditional values will enable you to overcome both treachery and your fears of failure.

6 Current difficulties will be resolved. You will experience the joy of triumph.

HEAVEN

OVER

FIRE

13 GATHERING

A gathering in the field.
Sign of the Sacrifice.
Auspicious to cross the great stream.
Good omen for the gentleman.

1 A gathering at the gate.
   No troubles.

2 A gathering at the ancestral temple.
   Trouble.

3 Soldiers in the grass, lying in ambush.
   Ascend to those high hills.
   They shall not rise for three years.

4 The city wall is scaled, but not won.
   It's time to attack.

5 The assemblage first wept, then laughed.
   The great armies finally clash.

6 A gathering at a ritual in the field.
   No grudges.

COMMENTARY

The images presented in this hexagram are of a city under siege. What is emphasized here is the importance of political unity and social coherence. Citizens can join together to seek safe refuge. Strong leadership, clarity of purpose, communication, and commitment to common values preserve the city, so that even though protective walls are breached, the city does not fall.

THE JUDGMENT Strong leadership at the head of a united and committed group can accomplish great things.

THE LINES 1 People are beginning to gather together, although they are not facing a threat.

2 Family gatherings can bring up underlying tensions and give way to quarrels.

3 External problems and pressures are beginning to take shape. If the signs are recognized early, preventive measures can be taken.

4 Your defenses have been breached. It is high time that you strike back.

5 Fears give way to confidence as you confront the enemy.

6 It is time to make peace and to let go of past bitterness.

FIRE

OVER

HEAVEN

14 GREAT HARVEST

Sign of the Great Sacrifice.

1 Make no cause for mutual harm, nor ill will.
   Come hard times, there should be no enmity.

2 Going somewhere in a big carriage.
   Safe and sound.

3 The Duke pays tribute to the Emperor.
   Common folks cannot do that.

4 Burn the rainmaker.
   No blame.

5 Punishment just, punishment firm.
   Good omen.

6 Blessed by Heaven.
   All goes well.

COMMENTARY

The harvest is an important occasion in China. It is a social exercise requiring cooperation from all, and its products are the staples that sustain life. This hexagram reads like a benediction, calling down the blessings of Heaven to the person who is aware of his role and responsibility in the social order.

THE JUDGMENT

This is a beneficent hexagram, befitting the most important ritual sacrifice of the agricultural year—the Great Harvest.

THE LINES

1 Cementing relationships during good times ensures an absence of enmity when the times turn bad.

2 You are transported safely and in style to your destination.

3 You are part of a larger social order, one that has well-defined roles and responsibilities for each person.

4 It was customary to sacrifice (burn) the rainmaker in times of drought, not only as punishment for his failure to produce results, but also as a propitiatory sacrifice to induce Heaven to send rain. If someone fails in his responsibility, it is just and proper to remove him.

5 It bodes well for an organization to maintain firm and just discipline.

6 All undertakings characterized by a sociable spirit will have the blessing of Heaven and will prosper.

EARTH

OVER

MOUNTAIN

15 MODESTY

Sign of the Sacrifice.
A gentleman comes to good end.

1 Modest, modest gentleman,
Crossing the great stream.
All goes well.

2 Known for modesty.
Good omen.

3 Achieving in modesty.
A gentleman comes to good end.

4 There is everything to gain
By practicing modesty.

5 Losing wealth, on account of a neighbor.
Attack brings success.

6 Known for modesty.
Auspicious to take military action,
To pacify the provinces.

COMMENTARY

MODESTY is the only hexagram in all of the I Ching to have six favorable lines, a strong indication of the high value tradition places on this virtue. It is interesting to note, however, that Chinese modesty differs from the western notion of humility or Christian meekness. Modesty is a code of proper behavior in social intercourse. It is also strategically useful, for it can mask one's motives and ambitions.

THE JUDGMENT   Observing social rules will bring rewards.

THE LINES

1   A person of great decorum is favored to undertake important projects.

2   A reputation for modesty bodes well for future activities.

3   Getting to the top in a decorous way enables you to enjoy the fruits of success.

4   Modesty is the best policy.

5   Aggressive action is justified and effective if one has suffered losses at the hands of a bad neighbor. Here the bad neighbor clearly refers to the Shang, whom the Zhou attacked and overthrew in righteousness.

6   A reputation for modesty is favorable for those who have to undertake aggressive action.

THUNDER

OVER

EARTH

16 WEARINESS

Auspicious to appoint helpers,
To take military action.

1	Weary amidst fame. Misfortune.
2	Hard as rock, but not all day. Good omen.
3	Weary at sunrise. Tardiness brings regrets.
4	Weary at play. There will be big gains. Be not suspicious of friendly gossip.
5	Sign for a long illness: No death.
6	Weary at night. The city wall crumbles. No troubles.

COMMENTARY

This is the hexagram for those who suffer a malaise of the spirit, fatigue of the heart. Life seems endlessly bland, boring, useless, dull. Lacking passion, one treads on wearily; nothing satisfied, delights, or pleases. Fame, success, play, friendships are dry as dust, devoid of meaning, empty. Work alone can keep us afloat during this dry spell. It is appropriate to get the help we need and to organize our forces to move forward when the wind changes and the time is right.

THE JUDGMENT

The time to get assistance is when you feel weary; this can help you to break out of the lethargy.

THE LINES

1 When you are in public life, any lapse in conduct can bring disfavor.

2 You should be firm, but at the same time maintain a degree of flexibility.

3 As a Chinese proverb says: "The key to the year is Spring. The key to the day is morning; and that to one's life, diligence." There is no room for weariness at the start.

4 A Chinese proverb again comes to mind: "A career is honed by diligence, and wasted in play." You should be serious and ignore criticism for being unsociable.

5 A long illness drags on but does not end in death.

6 You feel too tired to maintain your defenses, but no harm will come now if you let your guard down.

LAKE

OVER

THUNDER

17 THE CHASE

Sign of the Great Sacrifice.
Auspicious omen.
No troubles.

1 A house damaged.
Good omen.
Get out and achieve.

2 Holding the boy and losing the man.

3 Holding the man and losing the boy.
Give chase and get what you sought.
Good omen for settling down.

4 Falling into a trap during the chase.
Unfortunate omen.
On the open road punishments await,
To expose the guilty.

5 A penalty drink at the banquet.
Good omen.

6 Imprisoned first, then set free,
The King makes offerings at West Mountain.*

*King Wen of Zhou was imprisoned by the evil Shang Emperor Jou for seven years, during which time he purportedly created the hexagrams of the I Ching. His son King Wu overthrew the Shang, founded the Zhou Dynasty, and installed the I Ching as its official oracle. (See Chapter 2.)

COMMENTARY

Dissatisfaction with present conditions can be a strong motivation to great achievement. This is about the obstacles we must face in pursuing a goal. We are apt to make mistakes and transgressions, and it is hard to follow the right path, for choosing one forecloses another. At times it may seem that for every gain there is a countervailing loss. Nevertheless, the hexagram is sympathetic and generally encouraging.

THE JUDGMENT

A favorable hexagram for even the most ambitious of plans.

THE LINES

1   Setbacks that provoke you into action can prove favorable in the long run.

2   You cannot have things both ways; making a choice means abandoning its alternative.

3   It may seem as if you are mistaken no matter what you choose, but this is not so. You can obtain what you seek, and you should settle down to enjoy it once it has been obtained.

4   Your quest is temporarily halted by an obstacle. The setback can serve the purpose of exposing your weaknesses and faults, so that you may correct them.

5   A moment of camaraderie and joviality. Taking an extra drink of wine as a forfeit in a drinking game was done frequently in good fun and in the company of good friends.

6   You have survived setbacks. Give thanks and prepare to fight again.

MOUNTAIN

OVER

WIND

18 WORK

Sign of the Great Sacrifice.
Auspicious to cross the great stream,
Three days before the first,
Three days after the first.

1 Taking up the father's work.
With a son, the father is at ease.
Through danger, all ends well.

2 Taking up the mother's work.
Inappropriate.

3 Taking up the father's work.
There will be small regrets,
But no big mistakes.

4 Obstructing the father's work.
Seeing him brings acrimony.

5 Taking up the father's work.
Fame comes.

6 Serve not the mighty.
Keep your goals lofty.*

---

*This is a famous line, and it embodies the romantic ideal of the philosopher hermit, who, in spite of his superior learning and talents, deigns not to cast his lot with the mundane world—unless a truly noble cause beckons. A relevant example was Lu Wang, known to later ages as Old Master Jiang, who was sought out from his retreat by King Wen of Zhou. Lu Wang became Chief-of-Staff to King Wen's successor, King Wu, and engineered the successful campaign to overthrow the Shang Dynasty. (See Chapter 2.)

COMMENTARY

In this hexagram we see the eternal struggle between father and son, tradition and innovation, the old order and the new. Work is the focal point of these tensions, and it serves as the medium in which the conflict is to be resolved. This hexagram suggests that the conflict is resolved by coming to terms with the father and by establishing high personal standards of integrity.

THE JUDGMENT

Important undertakings are favored, but timing is critical.

THE LINES

1   A father wants his son to follow in his footsteps. It gives him a sense of immortality.

2   Work that appeals to the more passive side of your personality will not allow the fullest expression of your abilities.

3   A conservative approach offers the best protection from error, though you may not feel completely fulfilled.

4   Denying your true vocation brings discord to the family.

5   If you can be happy and content with traditional values, you will be rewarded by society.

6   It is important to maintain your own standards of integrity in your work and to resist pressures from above.

EARTH

OVER

LAKE

19 PREVAILING

Sign of the Great Sacrifice.
Auspicious omen.
Misfortune in the eighth month.

| | 1 | Prevailing through persuasion.
Good omen. |

1   Prevailing through persuasion.
Good omen.

2   Prevailing through persuasion.
All goes well.
No obstacles.

3   Prevailing by force.
Nothing is gained.
If softening follows,
There will be no grudge.

4   Prevailing through sincerity.
Faultless.

5   Prevailing through reason
Becomes a great king.
All goes well.

6   Prevailing through honesty.
All goes well. Faultless.

COMMENTARY

The main concern of this hexagram is the art of gaining influence over people. The advice is directed toward a leader of the people, in particular the King. Persuasion through honesty and sincerity is very much favored, and the use of force discouraged.

THE JUDGMENT

Conditions are favorable now. But your influence cannot last forever.

THE LINES

1 Influence people by persuading them.

2 The importance of persuasion as a technique to gain power is underscored.

3 The use of force is counterproductive—its damage should be contained by making amends.

4 No one can find fault with sincere means.

5 It is particularly important that a person with absolute power be guided by reason rather than whim.

6 Persuasion must be done with honesty.

WIND

OVER

EARTH

20 VIEW

The libation is made,
But the offering is withheld.*
Great punishment will befall.

1 Viewing through a child's eye.
   Blameless for common folks,
   Wrong for a gentleman.

2 Viewing from behind a screen.
   Good omen for a maiden.

3 Viewing my life:
   Advances, retreats.

4 Viewing the country's glory.
   Auspicious to visit the King.

5 Viewing my life:
   A gentleman should be faultless.

6 Viewing other's lives:
   A gentleman should be faultless.

*Ancient ritual sacrifices consisted of two parts: a libation (pouring of wine into the ground) and a sacrifice (offering of foods). Performing one act without the other was sacrilege, certain to call down the wrath of Heaven.

COMMENTARY

This hexagram shows us the different ways a person might see things: through the eyes of a child, a maiden, a gentleman. The external world offers rich visual experiences, but introspection is the most important view of all, for it enables us to see our strengths and weaknesses, successes and failures. We must strive to realize an ideal self-image.

THE JUDGMENT

It is of the utmost importance to complete undertakings. Failing to follow through will bring disastrous consequences.

THE LINES

1 Naiveté may be charming, but it is unacceptable for someone in a position of responsibility.

2 High-born women in ancient China generally did not appear in public. They could participate in court and ceremonial functions from behind a screen, which necessarily limits the view but on the other hand offers protection from the glare of the public. Such a compromise is appropriate for one leading a sheltered life.

3 Introspection brings a realization of the joys and sorrows of life.

4 A diplomatic emissary views the glory that was Shang—the Great Kingdom—and presents his credentials to the King.

5 In contemplating your life, it is essential to be able to judge your conduct as having been free of fault.

6 The standards of correct conduct are equally obligatory for all. It is appropriate to judge others by your own standards.

FIRE

OVER

THUNDER

21 BITING

Sign of the Sacrifice.
Favorable to invoke the law.

1 Dragging leg irons:
Toes invisible.
No harm comes.

2 Biting into meat:
Nose invisible.
No harm comes.

3 Biting into preserved meat,
Finding poison:
A small inconvenience.
No harm done.

4 Biting into dried ribs,
Finding a golden arrowhead:
Good omen in hardship.
All's well.

5 Biting into dried meat,
Finding gold:
Danger. No harm done.*

6 Wearing neck irons:
Ears invisible.
Disaster.

*It was believed that swallowing gold can cause death.

COMMENTARY

嗞嗑

The image of the hexagram itself portrays an open mouth with an obstruction between the teeth, like a bit in a horse's mouth. It is a metaphor for constriction, restraint, imprisonment. The hexagram is about the attempt to free ourselves by symbolically "biting off" the offending obstruction. In so doing, we find ourselves biting into different things at various times. Overall, warning is given that the restraints grow progressively and, if not counteracted, will eventually result in complete engulfment. The message is that one must "bite the bullet" and throw off the restraints before they become overwhelming.

THE JUDGMENT Invoking the law here means punishing the guilty. If you are innocent, you are safe even if falsely confined.

THE LINES

1 At first the restraint came in a minor way and caused no alarm.

2 You are up to your nose in problems and must fight to free yourself.

3 "Chewing over" old bitterness can poison the atmosphere.

4 Finding the arrowhead signifies that you have hacked deep into the problem.

5 There is danger in the places one seeks nourishment, but watchfulness prevents harm.

6 If the restraints are allowed to pile up progressively, you will become completely imprisoned.

MOUNTAIN

OVER

FIRE

22 DECORATION

Sign of the Sacrifice.
Somewhat auspicious to go somewhere.

1 Decorating the foot,
Leaving the carriage to walk.

2 Decorating the beard.

3 Luxuriant beard,
With dew besmeared.
Good omen everlasting.

4 Mottled white, horses bright.
They're not robbers, only wife grabbers.

5 The garden is all decked out.
No presents to speak about.
Awkward, but all ends well.

6 Decorating on white.
Faultless.

COMMENTARY

A whimsical note marks this uncharacteristic hexagram, which invokes a series of images related to a wedding. The common thread running through the lines is ornamentation. Being a festive occasion, a wedding is a time when a little vanity is acceptable and niggardliness reproachable. The hexagram ends on a serene and hopeful note for a new beginning.

THE JUDGMENT

Enthusiasm for a new undertaking is tempered by a diffident note. This is not surprising, as the hexagram relates to a wedding, which the I Ching usually approaches with caution and ambivalence.

THE LINES

1 Wearing foot ornaments and leaving the carriage to walk barefoot suggests exuberance. (The groom is ecstatic.)

2 Cultivating a beard requires an inordinate degree of care and suggests a certain vanity. (The groom is preening himself.)

3 A luxuriant beard is sign of vigor and longevity, and the dew signifies good fortune. (The I Ching often regards rain as a good omen.)

4 Ornamented horses used in a ritualistic abduction of the bride by the groom's party convey a sense of merriment and celebration.

5 The bride's family decorated the garden beautifully for the wedding, but the groom brought only niggardly gifts. However, this discordant note was eventually smoothed over.

6 This presents the image of a new beginning, perhaps the arrival of a baby.

MOUNTAIN

OVER

EARTH

23 LOSS

Do not go anywhere.

1 Hitting the bed with the foot.
The dream bodes ill.

2 Hitting the bed with the knee,
The dream bodes ill.

3 Hit it. No fault.

4 Hitting the bed with the shoulder.
Misfortune.

5 Using a eunuch as servant.
No objection to intimate trust.

6 Refusing a fat plum.
The gentleman gains a carriage.
The common man loses his house.

COMMENTARY

The progression of a nightmare seems to leave the dreamer feeling helpless and frustrated, but in fact it serves as a warning. If heeded, it will save the sleeper from imminent danger. The ending line tells us, rather cynically, that things are never what they seem. Taken as a whole, the hexagram warns against any kind of activity. Striking out or acting out will not accomplish anything and may even result in greater misfortune. The only grace note is the presence of an assistant or friend who can be trusted. The story of Prince Hai forms the backdrop for the lines, though he is never explicitly mentioned. (See Chapter 2 and 56 THE TRAVELER.)

THE JUDGMENT

A time of loss is a time for consolidation, not for overt action.

THE LINES

1   We have the image of a fitful sleeper. He tosses and turns, hits the bed with his foot, and is having a foreboding nightmare. Things do not look well.

2   The sleeper turns restless. The nightmare becomes more ominous, and there is no sign of abatement.

3   It is alright to hit the bed during fitful sleep; it might awaken the sleeper from his nightmare.

4   Tossing and turning too violently during a nightmare causes injury to the sleeper.

5   Eunuchs were employed to manage the imperial palace because they could be trusted not to engage in improper liaisons. This line recalls Prince Hai's trustworthy servant. (See 56 THE TRAVELER.)

6   The same action can lead to quite different consequences, depending on one's station in life. Refusing a reward can enrich a successful man but impoverish an average one. The former gains in reputation; the latter loses a much-needed source of funds.

EARTH

OVER

THUNDER

24 RETURN

Sign of the Sacrifice.
No illness at home or abroad.
Friends come in peace.
On the road back and forth,
Seven days to return.
Auspicious to go somewhere.

1 Returning from a short trip.
No big troubles.
All's well.

2 Returning joyfully.
All's well.

3 Returning with a frown.
Danger. No harm.

4 Returning alone in mid-journey.

5 Returning angrily.
No regrets.

6 Returning after losing one's way.
Misfortune. Trouble is in store.
Taking arms will lead to great defeat,
And disaster for the King.
For ten years the conquest will not succeed.

COMMENTARY

This marks a turning point where opposites collide. Timing is essential. One must "seize the hour" in order to make progress. There is danger that one might let the right moment slip by without taking advantage of it. A lost opportunity may lead to longstanding setbacks.

THE JUDGMENT

Fortune is smiling. You have health, friends, purpose, and time on your side. You should be able to accomplish great things.

THE LINES

1 The situation is about to change for the better.

2 Your endeavor has been successfully discharged, and you are free now to savor your success.

3 Things are not perfect. There is an element of danger that may prove disruptive, but no real harm will come to you.

4 Companions have proven to be disappointing. Remaining true to yourself, you part company and go your own way.

5 Even though you are angered, you have no regrets about the decision you made. Stick to your guns!

6 Straying from the right path will result in a long-lasting setback. Aggressive action will only deepen your woes.

HEAVEN

OVER

THUNDER

25 PROPRIETY

Sign of the Great Sacrifice.
Auspicious omen.
If anything is improper, woe will befall.
It would be unfavorable to go anywhere.

1 Go only with propriety.
   All's well.

2 If you can reap without planting,
   Resow without fallow,
   Then go ahead.

3 There once was a careless fire,
   Started perchance by a cow.
   The passersby took everything,
   To the loser's wail and howl.

4 Possibly auspicious.
   No troubles.

5 An expected illness
   Needs no medicine to cure.

6 Improper action brings woes.
   Nothing will be gained.

COMMENTARY

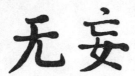

The Natural Order ordains what is fitting and proper for every situation. Thus, one should not expect gains without labor, and one should take precautions to safeguard one's property. Conduct that is at odds with the Natural Order will only bring woes.

THE JUDGMENT

To get somewhere, you are admonished to follow a straight and narrow path.

THE LINES

1 You must approach people in an appropriate manner.

2 In order to get results, you have to do the required work.

3 This line doubtless relates a popular story of the time in the form of a homespun rhyme, to warn against carelessness.

4 Cautious optimism prevails.

5 An illness or ill event brought about by your own willful misconduct cannot be cured by medicine, but rather by a change of heart and a subsequent change in behavior.

6 Impropriety will bring woes in the end, even though it might seem to work at first.

MOUNTAIN

OVER

HEAVEN

26 BIG CATTLE

Auspicious omen.
Do not dine at home.
Auspicious to cross the great stream.

1 Danger.
You will profit.

2 The wheel falls off the cart.

3 Giving chase on a good steed.
Good omen for hard times.
The team and the chariot are ready.
Auspicious to go somewhere.

4 Curbing the calf's horns.
Great auspicious omen.

5 Fencing in the gelded pig.
Auspicious omen.

6 Blessed by Heaven.
Sign of the Sacrifice.

COMMENTARY

Farming images convey an expansive vision, urging us to take action, go somewhere, do something. The dominant note is positive: Proper preparation saves us from danger and permits us to expand both our possessions and horizons.

THE JUDGMENT

The time to act is now. Your endeavors will meet with a positive response. Be bold in moving beyond the familiar and comfortable.

THE LINES

1   Danger brings opportunities.

2   Faulty equipment causes setbacks.

3   Go on the offensive, undaunted by hardship. The means to prevail are available to you.

4   A calf's horns can inflict damage on people and property. Curbing them is a wise preventive measure.

5   Gelded pigs produced fatter profits in the marketplace. Guard what is most precious.

6   Heaven helps those who help themselves.

MOUNTAIN

OVER

THUNDER

27 THE CHEEKS

Auspicious omen.
Seeing a filled cheek,
One seeks food for oneself.

1 You leave your delectable turtle
To stare at my bulging cheeks.
Misfortune.

2 Cheeks bulging.
Bashing a leg against the hillside.
Advancing brings disaster.

3 A slap on the cheek.
Misfortune.
For ten years, incapacity.
Nothing will be gained.

4 Cheeks bulging.
Tiger staring, staring hard.
Desire running, running wild.
Blameless.

5 Bashing a leg.
Settle down.
Do not cross the great stream.

6 A pat on the cheek.
Safe in peril.
Auspicious to cross the great stream.

COMMENTARY

Self-nourishment is our fundamental responsibility. It involves not only the food we eat, but our thoughts and the care we take of all the dimensions in our lives. Paying too much attention to what others have leads to self-pity and discontent. Envy becomes like a ravenous tiger ready to devour and destroy. Envy and greed end in disaster, but healthy desire, which seeks only to nourish the self, merits an approving pat on the cheek.

THE JUDGMENT

Seeing others well-provided for inspires a desire for self-improvement. This is a healthy drive, as long as you are careful to seek the proper nourishment.

THE LINES

1 You are ignoring the delicious meal on your own plate and thinking of what others have. Such envy brings misfortune.

2 Seeking more when you are already full brings harm.

3 Stinging reprimands bring your life to a halt. Spiritual and physical neglect have rendered you incapable of acting.

4 Unbridled covetousness, though understandable, becomes ominous. (The phrase about the staring tiger has become a standard metaphor for an aggressive country eyeing a weak neighbor as a choice morsel to be had.)

5 Injuries can be healed by rest and proper nourishment.

6 Approval brings security. It is a good time for big undertakings.

LAKE

OVER

WIND

28 GREAT EXCESS

The column is bent.
It is better to go somewhere.
Sign of the Sacrifice.

1   The offering is wrapped in white palm.
Faultless.

2   The withered willow sprouts leaves.
The old man gets a young wife.
Everything goes well.

3   The column is bent.
Misfortune.

4   Tall columns.
Good omen.
But beware of snakes.

5   The withered willow blossoms.
The old woman gets a young husband.
No blame, no praise.

6   Overreaching during crossing.
Water overhead.
Disaster.

COMMENTARY

This hexagram takes as its motif the basic method of construction used in Chinese architecture. All dwellings use poles to support a roof. As buildings become more grand and opulent, the size, girth, and grandeur of the poles grow until they become massive, decorative columns. The stronger and straighter the column, the more secure and elaborate the building. Thus, a bent column is a serious concern, for it presages the imminent collapse of the roof and consequently of the whole building. A column might bend under extraordinary pressure, or because of its own inferior qualities or construction. Overreaching the limits of any person or situation may result in disaster.

THE JUDGMENT

If the situation is inherently flawed, it is better to remove yourself from it to avoid the imminent collapse.

THE LINES

1   Ancestral offerings consisted of food wrapped in white palm leaves. The ritual offerings had to be made properly in order to be acceptable.

2   An unlikely alliance may produce fruit. A rejuvenation of the spirit is likely to follow.

3   The support necessary for your undertakings is inadequate and your project may be jeopardized as a consequence.

4   There may be ulterior motives or hidden dangers in the source of your support. The situation looks promising, but read the fine print.

5   Things appear unseasonably bright. An old woman might blossom with the love of a younger man, but she still would not be able to bear fruit.

6   There is a temptation to overextend yourself. Resist it, for it will lead to disaster.

WATER

OVER

WATER

29 WATER

Faith ties the heart.
Sign of the Sacrifice.
To travel brings rewards.

1 A pit within a pit.
Falling into the pit,
Into the inner pit.
Disaster.

2 The pit holds danger.
Seek small gains.

3 Coming to the very pit,
A deep and dangerous pit.
Falling into the pit.
Trapped. Incapacitated.

4 Wine in the right glass
Is set beside the right plate.
And the bride comes through the door.
All ends well.

5 The pit you cannot fill,
Even by leveling a hill.
No fault.

6 Tied with ropes,
Thrown amongst thorns,
Undelivered for three years.
Disaster.

COMMENTARY

Speaking eloquently of the darkest moments of our lives, this hexagram plumbs the depths of doubt and desperation. Graphic images are used to convey feelings of being trapped, abandoned, bound, and incapacitated. Faith alone ties the heart to life and provides strength to endure until that moment when anticipation becomes fulfillment, suffering yields to satisfaction, and darkness turns to light.

THE JUDGMENT

You are setting out on a journey to find something. The mission will be successful only if you have faith.

THE LINES

1 Your troubles never seem to end. Things keep getting worse. The dangers are real, but inner doubts will lead to disaster.

2 There are real and present dangers at hand. Curb your ambitions for the moment.

3 You have come face to face with what you fear most, and you are being engulfed by it.

4 Decorous behavior enhances a joyous occasion. This anticipates the consummation and fulfillment that lie ahead.

5 The problem is so vast and overwhelming that it can never be resolved in spite of your most strenuous efforts. There is no blame in this.

6 When your hands are tied, there is nothing you can do but wait things out.

FIRE

OVER

FIRE

30 FIRE

Auspicious omen.
Sign of the Sacrifice.
Auspicious to keep a cow.

1   Gilded shoes.
    Be respectful, and be safe.

2   A yellow wild beast.
    Great auspicious omen.

3   A wild beast is seen during an eclipse.
    Clang the cymbal and sing,*
    Lest harm befalls the old.
    Misfortune.

4   Expelled.
    Returned.
    Burned.
    Died.
    Abandoned.

5   Weeping a stream,
    Crying a storm.
    All's well.

6   The King waged war,
    And offered rewards for heads.
    The wrong captives were taken.
    No fault.

*It was believed that lunar eclipses were caused by a "heavenly dog" devouring the moon. This led to
the custom of noise-making to save the moon by scaring away the beast.

COMMENTARY

The dual nature of fire—protector and destroyer—epitomizes the extreme swings of fortune described in the hexagram. The most gilded of positions gives way to utter degradation. The Chinese text is stark and dramatic as it expresses the extreme suffering of line 4. Emotional catharsis is restorative, but the cycle ends, not with a return to glory, but on a note of indifference.

THE JUDGMENT

Compliance with the shifts of fortune assures survival. Symbol of docility, a cow was also an important capital reserve for farmers.

THE LINES

1   Those who hold elevated positions must be respectful of people and of the tide of events, for the sake of self-preservation.

2   Yellow, sign of harmony, symbolizes the coming of great good fortune.

3   You should take steps to protect the elders from impending harm.

4   Your darkest fears will have to be faced.

5   Giving full expression to sorrow will be restorative.

6   In the scramble for power and wealth, understandably some mistakes are inevitable.

LAKE

OVER

MOUNTAIN

31 CUTTING

Sign of the Sacrifice.
Auspicious omen.
Favorable for taking a wife.

1   Cutting the big toe.

2   Cutting the calf.
Misfortune.
Stay home.

3   Cutting the thigh,
Guarding the wound.
Going brings woes.

4   Good omen.
Regret disappears.
Footsteps come, footsteps go.
Friends be with you.

5   Cutting the back.
No regrets.

6   Cutting the cheek, the tongue.

COMMENTARY

The taut construction and singular imagery of this hexagram derive power from the consistent repetition of a single character, the name of the hexagram, translated as chopping or cutting. The modern meaning of this character is "feeling" or "resonance," but the archaic meaning is derived from the original pictographic shape of an ax. The lines describe progressive wounds, each a little more serious, as they move from the big toe to the cheeks and tongue. There is a purposefulness to this damage, for it serves to limit one's activities. Although the hexagram is generally favorable, its specific lines warn against going somewhere, doing something, and even saying too much. It advises one to stay close to home, using one's time to heal and mend, enjoying the company of true friends.

THE JUDGMENT

The hexagram is generally favorable, particularly so for relationships and partnerships.

THE LINES

1 A warning to go no further with your plans.

2 You have gotten more involved in a situation than is safe. It would be better to remove yourself from the scene.

3 You are deeply hurt. It is time to rest and let the wounds heal.

4 The situation has changed for the better. People may come and go, events move on, but real friends remain.

5 Ending an involvement without regrets.

6 Be careful of sharp words and cutting conversations.

THUNDER

OVER

WIND

32 STEADFASTNESS

Sign of the Sacrifice.
No troubles.
Auspicious omen.
Auspicious for going somewhere.

1 Dredging constantly.
Omen of misfortune.
There is nothing to be gained.

2 Regret disappears.

3 Unsteadfastness in conduct
Could bring one shame.
Omen of difficulty.

4 No game is bagged in the hunt.

5 Steadfastness in conduct
Bodes well for a woman,
Ill for a man.

6 Agitating steadfastly.
Misfortune.

COMMENTARY

The sense of this hexagram is that steadfastness is a subtle art. We are apt to make the mistake of holding on to the wrong thing or the wrong person for too long and then, upon realizing this, overcorrecting the problem.

THE JUDGMENT

This is a good hexagram, as befits a ritual occasion. One who holds steadfastness in proper balance will have no troubles and will go places.

THE LINES

1 The image is that of someone constantly dredging up the past. Such diligence is wasted, for all you get is mud.

2 Progress is made by loosening the heavy grip of the past.

3 Unreliable behavior could determine your reputation and create further problems.

4 Without a certain amount of discipline, you will not get what you seek.

5 Because of social mores, a woman will always find it advantageous to be circumspect in her conduct; a man may find it necessary to be somewhat more aggressive and adaptable.

6 Making a fuss constantly, even for a good cause, leads to failure.

HEAVEN

OVER

MOUNTAIN

33 THE LITTLE PIG

Sign of the Sacrifice.
Auspicious for small things.

1 A little pig's tail.
Danger.
Do not go anywhere.

2 Tied with ox leather,
It cannot even struggle.
Let it loose.

3 A little pig tied.
There is danger of illness.
Hire servants.

4 A gift of ham.*
Appropriate for a gentleman,
Not for common folks.

5 A suckling pig is served at a gala.
Good omen.

6 A fat little pig.
Everything goes.

*Ham was a lavish and special gift in ancient China. Yang Hu, a powerful politician who wanted to persuade a reluctant Confucius to serve under him, sent Confucius a gift of ham when Confucius was out of the house (and hence could not be present to refuse it). By social custom, the significant gift obliged Confucius to pay Yang Hu a return visit. (As it turned out, Confucius waited till Yang Hu went out before calling on him, but unfortunately bumped into Yang Hu on the way and was trapped.)

COMMENTARY

The little pig evokes images of celebration and festive feasts. The hexagram assures us that self-help and assistance from competent people will enable us to overcome minor obstacles. We shall then be able to celebrate life in seemly fashion.

THE JUDGMENT

Realistic goals can be met.

THE LINES

1 Pig raisers in old China believed that cutting off a pig's tail would make it grow fatter. Here the little pig turns tail in fright to avoid such danger.

2 Tying the little pig with ox hide is unnecessary and will only hurt it. As a metaphor, this line advises us to release ourselves from self-imposed fears and worries.

3 You are incapacitated by illness, as a little pig is tied down by rope. You need to hire competent help.

4 In ancient China, giving ham was a grand gesture reserved for people of position. Common folks could not afford it, nor would it have been appropriate. Tailor your conduct to your station and means.

5 It is important to celebrate significant events and noteworthy achievements with all due ceremony.

6 A fat little pig is good for eating, giving, or sacrificial offering—a symbol of delightful rewards.

THUNDER

OVER

HEAVEN

34 GREAT INJURY

Auspicious omen.

1 Injury in the foot.
Advancing brings misfortune.
Punishment is in store.

2 Good omen.

3 For common folks, injury.
For the gentleman, anxiety.
Omen of danger.

4 The ram butts against the fence.
If its horns are curbed,
Then all goes well, regret disappears.
If the horns remain uncurbed
After the fence is broken,
Damage will befall the big cart's wheel.

5 He lost his sheep in the Kingdom of Yi.
No regrets.*

6 The ram butts against the fence.
It can neither advance nor retreat.
There is nothing to be gained.
Belt-tightening is indicated.

*This refers to the legendary Prince Hai, inventor of the ox yoke. (See his story in Chapter 2.)

COMMENTARY

Prince Hai, ancestor of the Shang people, inventor of the ox yoke, led an adventurous life. Settled in an alien land, he made and lost fortunes many times over and suffered the ultimate injury of being killed for his oxen by the local king. Here, however, our attention is directed to how he rebounded from setbacks time and again to rebuild a flourishing herd.

In spite of the ominous nature of some of the lines in this hexagram, its message is an optimistic one. Danger is real and imminent, but we can take preventive and protective action. What is important is flexibility, resilience, and perseverance.

THE JUDGMENT

Injury can serve as a warning, which can save you from greater harm.

THE LINES

1 The first steps have met with resistance. Continued action at this time would only bring further detriment.

2 The situation is now favorable.

3 The situation is dangerous. Followers get hurt, and leaders are anxious.

4 Don't keep hitting your head against a stone wall. Channel your energies to attainable goals.

5 A lesson from the story of Prince Hai: He did not waste time bemoaning his loss, but instead concentrated on rebuilding his herd.

6 Like the ram whose horns became locked in the fence it was butting against, you are so fenced in by some situations that there is no room to maneuver. Accept what cannot be changed and persevere until conditions become more favorable.

FIRE

OVER

EARTH

35 ADVANCE

Marquis Kang presents a herd of horses,
The spoils of three victories in a day.*

1 Advancing, conquering.
Good omen.
No captives taken.
Yet, no blame.

2 Advancing, menacing.
Good omen.
Largess from the Queen Mother.

3 The people approve.
Regret disappears.

4 Advancing like a mouse.
Omen of danger.

5 Regret disappears.
What is lost will be found.
Fear not, it's favorable to go.
Nothing stands in the way.

6 The spearhead advances
To take a city.
Perilous but safe.
Blameless but pointless.

*Marquis Kang was a younger son of King Wen, who created the hexagrams. The Marquis's elder brother King Wu overthrew the Shang and became the first emperor of the Zhou Dynasty. (See Chapter 2.) The "Kang Cauldron," an inscribed bronze cauldron commemorating the endowment of his fief, is considered one of the important relics of the Zhou Dynasty.

COMMENTARY

Marquis Kang is seen here as a man of style, if not necessarily of substance. The secret of his success lay in his ability to play to the crowds, put up a good front, and appear to be more menacing and dangerous than in fact he was. In war as in life, appearance may matter more than substance, not only to the easily manipulated masses, but to those with the power to reward as well.

THE JUDGMENT

The Marquis dutifully presents the spoils of war to his King. This hexagram shows us the efficacy of "rendering unto Caesar." Punctilious, respectful conduct can further your fortunes.

THE LINES

1 With great fanfare the army is led forward. There is great show but no real victory.

2 A greater show of force wins the approval of those in power, particularly those most inclined to be impressed by display.

3 There is great popular support for this campaign, and any regret about the real hollowness of victory disappears in the face of such enthusiasm.

4 Presenting a bold front is wildly applauded—acting stealthily or timidly would be dangerous.

5 Whatever is truly yours can never be lost, for it will always find its way back into your life.

6 A show of strength for its own sake involves some calculated risks. Be careful to distinguish form from substance when confronted with opposition.

EARTH

OVER

FIRE

36 THE CRYING PHEASANT

Good omen for one in hardship.

─────────── 1 The crying pheasant is flying,
Its wings drooping.
A gentleman is journeying,
For three days hungering.
One goes somewhere,
And is reproached by the host.

── ── 2 The crying pheasant is wounded in the left leg.
Good omen for castrating a horse.
It will be strong.

─────────── 3 The crying pheasant is flying.
Chasing it southward, he finds the main road.
For illness, no progress.

── ── 4 He enters the left valley,
And captures the crying pheasant.
Be careful about leaving home.

── ── 5 Jizi captures the crying pheasant.*
Good omen.

── ── 6 The pheasant stops crying.
Transition.
It soars to heaven,
Then plunges into water.**

*Jizi was prime minister to Jou the Terrible, last emperor of the Shang Dynasty (c. 1150 B.C.). He was much admired for his wisdom and courage. For admonishing Jou for his excesses, Jizi was thrown into prison and escaped execution only by feigning madness. After Jou was overthrown by King Wu, first emperor of the Zhou Dynasty and son of King Wen, who designed the hexagrams of the I Ching, Jizi was freed. Declining the opportunity to serve the new Zhou ruler, he migrated to the Kingdom of Chosen (Korea) and settled several thousand of his followers there. There is a tomb in Pyongyang bearing his name. (See Chapter 2.)

**This refers to a symbolism of seasonal change. It is said in Li Ji (Book of Rites), one of the Confucian classics, that to mark the beginning of winter in the tenth month, a pheasant plunges into the Great Water and transforms itself into a clam.

COMMENTARY

The image of the crying pheasant is used in three different ways: poetically, historically, and symbolically. It is a literary device used to create a certain mood; it is a bird hunted down successfully by Jizi; it is also a symbol of transformation. Perhaps there was a story, now lost, of Jizi chasing for days after a pheasant, enduring hunger and losing his way, but finally getting his prey. The lines of the hexagram follow a certain thread, but most end with an aside that is a specific response to certain questions.

THE JUDGMENT

This hexagram is about perseverance overcoming hardship.

THE LINES

1   The crying pheasant is a literary device to lead into the story of a man (presumably Jizi) journeying in hunger for three days.
Advice: If you go on a visit, you will be reproached by the host.

2   Jizi went after a pheasant and wounded it in the left leg. The chase probably started as a quest for food, but soon it took on a purpose of its own.
Advice (for farmers): Shooting a pheasant is a good omen for castrating a horse.

3   The pheasant, though wounded, kept flying. Jizi chased it southward and inadvertently got onto the main road (from which he had presumably strayed).
Advice (for those consulting about illness): No progress.

4   He finally got his bird, in the left valley.
Advice: Caution to travelers.

5   Reaffirmation of success: Jizi got the crying pheasant.
Advice: Good omen.

6   Our hero lost the pheasant at the very moment he captured it, for it was transformed into something else.

WIND

OVER

FIRE

37 THE FAMILY

Auspicious for a girl.

1 Guarding the home.
Regret disappears.

2 All is dandy in the pantry.
Auspicious.

3 The family agitating.
Danger is weathered.
Women and children tittering.
A sad end comes.

4 A wealthy family.
Great fortune.

5 The King comes to the house.
Fear not.
All goes well.

6 To be firm in punishment
Brings good in the end.

COMMENTARY

The unity of the family is expressed in its ordered relationships. Man is guardian, woman nurturer; but there is no primacy in these roles. What matters is that each individual fulfills his or her function so that the family may flourish as a whole. Frivolity is to be avoided, and discipline must be maintained.

THE JUDGMENT

A woman's road to success is clearly outlined.

THE LINES

1 Assuming responsibility brings rewards of certainty and self-satisfaction.

2 Nourishing the family is an act of love and a responsibility equal to that of guarding the home.

3 The Chinese original reproduces literal sound effects heard in a family: "Gao-gao" (sound of consternation) indicates a concerted effort to face a threat, and danger will be averted. "Hee-hee" (sounds of foolish laughter) betrays laxity, which will prove to be the family's undoing. Relationships can endure anything but disrespect.

4 Rich family life is one of life's greatest blessings.

5 Be calm and take advantage of the presence of an influential guest.

6 Firm and fair discipline is important in raising the kind of children you can be proud of.

FIRE

OVER

LAKE

38 ABANDONED

Favorable in small things.

1 Regret disappears.
Do not chase after the lost horse.
It will return of its own accord.
Seeing an evil person bodes no ill.

2 Meeting the host in the alley.
No troubles.

3 The cart: pulled from behind.
The ox: chafing.
The man: branded and defaced.*
Bad beginning, good end.

4 The abandoned waif met a great man.**
Both became prisoners.
Safe in peril.

5 Regret disappears.
They are munching meat in the ancestral temple.
Go. Who could blame you?

6 The abandoned waif saw a pig in the mud,
And a cart full of demons.
He arched his bow at first,
But finally put it down.
They are not robbers, only wife grabbers.***
Going would be favorable, if it rains.

---

*This describes a man who was criminally punished by having his face branded and nose cut off.
**The abandoned waif most probably refers to Shao Kang (Kang the Younger), posthumous son of King Xiang of the Xia Dynasty (the one just preceding the Shang, which preceded the Zhou). King Xiang was killed by a usurper of the throne. His pregnant queen escaped and gave birth to Shao Kang in exile. Shao Kang was kept on the run for some twenty years, hounded by his father's murderer. Eventually he returned triumphant to avenge his father and reclaim his throne. The story is told in more detail in Chapter 2.
***See note in hexagram 3 RETRENCHMENT.

COMMENTARY

In this hexagram we find snippets of some folklore about the Adventures of the Abandoned Waif. There is an ironic sense of humor and a farcical element in the account of the strange circumstances in which the waif had become enmeshed.

While we may sometimes perceive ourselves as friendless, hopeless, and abandoned, this hexagram reminds us that it is not so. What appears to be ominous can in fact be a good sign. Something that seems frightful and dangerous may turn out to be good fun. In the end, it is our attitude alone that prevails and shapes our destiny.

THE JUDGMENT   Keep your goals attainable and realistic.

THE LINES

1 Luck is with you. Your loss will be restored and frightening circumstances will cause you no harm.

2 Gracious and generous support may appear in unexpected or even hidden places.

3 This line describes a strange scene in which a branded criminal was engaged in a tug-of-war against an ox yoked to a cart. The sense is that your feeling of frustration and of being stalled may have been caused by the dishonesty or untrustworthiness of someone else. Being aware of this will liberate you.

4 You will find a companion who will sustain you in your trials and tribulations. You have much to share with each other.

5 It is time to leave the sorrows of the past behind you and join in the feast of life.

6 The situation is not what it appears to be. What seems frightening and dangerous may be just part of the pageantry of life.

WATER

OVER

MOUNTAIN

39 ADMONISHMENT

The southwest bodes well.
The northeast bodes ill.
Auspicious to see the great personage.
Good omen.

1   Giving admonishment,
    Receiving praise.

2   The King's minister admonishes fervently,
    Not for his own sake.

3   Giving admonishment,
    Receiving reproach.

4   Giving admonishment,
    Receiving an excuse.

5   Admonishing intensely,
    Acquiring a friend.

6   Giving admonishment,
    Acquiring confidence.
    All's well.
    Auspicious to see the great personage.

COMMENTARY

Giving advice is always difficult. It is a sensitive task at best, and at worst it can be a hazardous occupation, fraught with danger for the bearer of unwelcome truths. Chinese history abounds with tales of what befell imperial counselors who dared to tell the truth at their own peril. We see from history that an emperor's reaction to the admonition of his counselors depended more on his own personal inclination than on the strength or truth of the message.

This hexagram explores the varied reactions to advice given and complements hexagram 8 SUPPORT.

THE JUDGMENT

Some situations are better for you than others. This is a good time to seek advice from someone you respect.

THE LINES

1 The advice you gave others has proven helpful to them.

2 This line brings to mind the story of Prime Minister Jizi (hero of hexagram 36 THE CRYING PHEASANT), who admonished the last Shang emperor, Jou, for his terrible excesses. The advice given was for the good of the country, but Jizi was imprisoned for his efforts.

3 The advice you give may not always be well received or appreciated. You may even find yourself reproached for your efforts.

4 When people become defensive on receiving advice, their initial response is often to search for excuses for their behavior.

5 The friends who love you best are never afraid to speak the truth, no matter how painful or difficult it might be.

6 Following the wise counsel of a trusted advisor can give us a sense of strength and purpose and a feeling of confidence about our undertakings.

THUNDER

OVER

WATER

40 LETTING LOOSE

The southwest bodes well.
If there is nowhere to go,
You had better return.
If there is somewhere to go,
You had better make haste.

1   No troubles.

2   Getting three foxes in the hunt,
Finding a yellow arrowhead.
Good omen.

3   Riding in a loaded cart,
Attracting robbers.
Omen of difficulty.

4   The net you set was loosened.
Punish your friends when they come.

5   The gentleman loosened the rope.
Good for him.
The common folks got the punishment.*

6   The Duke aimed at an eagle from atop a high wall.
He got it.
Everything goes well.

*This line brings to mind a story about Lord Tang, founder of the Shang Dynasty. One day he went to the field and witnessed hunters closing in on their prey with nets from four sides. Tang ordered them to remove the nets on three sides, for in his dominion "only willing animals shall be taken." When people in the neighboring states heard about this, they all praised Lord Tang for his compassionate rule, which "benefited even the wild beasts."

COMMENTARY

解

Planning ahead is always a wise course of action, but even the best of organizers can never completely anticipate precisely what may happen. Sometimes we may have unexpected windfalls, but more often something goes wrong. Our friends may spoil our plans. Our actions may have unintended harmful consequences to others, even though we mean well. In the end, setting high goals is the best we can do, and it maximizes our chances of succeeding.

THE JUDGMENT

Do what you have to do, but "if it's not broken, don't fix it."

THE LINES

1 For the moment, you are free of worry.

2 There is unexpected good fortune, in addition to the good fortune you have won through your own efforts.

3 Success attracts hostility and envy. There are others who would seek to deprive you of your good fortune.

4 You may find that friends have altered your plans, and you will want to confront them about their interference.

5 A grand gesture is very well for the powers that be, but the underlings suffer its fallout.

6 Aiming high brings good fortune.

MOUNTAIN

OVER

LAKE

41 DECREASE

Punishment is in store.
Great fortune protects you.
Omen of feasibility.
Auspicious to go somewhere.
Food is delivered to the field
In two exquisite baskets,
Fit for sacrificial rites.*

1   On ceremonial occasions, go promptly.
No troubles.
Cut down on wine.

2   Auspicious omen.
But to advance brings misfortune.
Do not detract from it, nor enhance it.

3   If three persons go,
One will be lost.
If one person goes,
He will find his friend.

4   The illness subsides,
And soon heals.
No woes.

5   Someone is proffering a tortoise shell
Worth ten double cowries.**
It cannot be refused.
Great auspicious omen.

6   Do not detract from it, nor enhance it.
Blameless.
Good omen.
Auspicious to go somewhere.
You will gain a homeless servant.

*An official was forced to retire from office. Friends sent good wishes in the form of food for his journey home.

COMMENTARY

This hexagram urges us to a time of quietude and inactivity, emphasizing the importance of action through inaction. Twice it tells us neither to detract from nor to enhance the situation in which we find ourselves. When action is required, only the barest minimum of effort is recommended. This is seen to be an interim period of rest and renewal, perhaps after a setback in life. Soon we shall be ready to resume activities.

THE JUDGMENT

In general, what you do and where you go will be productive, and you will have the wherewithal necessary to perform the duties incumbent on your place in life. There is an element of grace and style in all your activities, no matter how simple or humble.

THE LINES

1   Be attentive to your duties and be temperate, prompt, and courteous in dealings with others.

2   Allow things to unfold in their own time and manner.

3   It is difficult to work with too many people. Join forces only with those you need to accomplish your goals.

4   If left to their own course, things can often heal themselves.

5   The offer of tortoise shells here symbolizes an opportunity you cannot afford to pass up, even if you did not want it.

6   The period of rest and renewal is coming to an end. A new and active phase is beginning, and you will get the help and support you need.

**Cowrie shells were strung in lots of twenty for use as currency. In Shang times, it cost twenty double cowries to commission the casting of a bronze cauldron. Thus ten double cowries must have been a princely sum.

WIND

OVER

THUNDER

42 INCREASE

Auspicious to go somewhere.
Auspicious to cross the great stream.

1   Favorable to start major construction.
    Great auspicious omen.
    No troubles.

2   Someone is proffering a tortoise shell
    Worth ten double cowries.*
    It cannot be refused.
    Everlasting good omen.
    The King offers a sacrifice to God.
    Good fortune.

3   Assistance offered at a disaster.
    Faultless. Trust gained.
    On the road, the Duke got the news by jade tablet.

4   On the road, the Duke got the news, agreed,
    And assisted in moving the Capital.

5   Trust gladdens the heart.
    Needless to ask, great fortune.
    Trust is our reward.

6   None will rally.
    Some will attack.
    If there is no determination in the heart,
    Disaster will befall.

*Ten double cowries represented a princely sum. (See note in 41 DECREASE.) Here it probably refers to the ransom paid by the Zhou state to secure the release of their King Wen, who had been falsely imprisoned by the evil Shang emperor Jou for seven years (during which time he created the hexagrams).

COMMENTARY

During one of the many floods that brought periodic havoc to the Shang kingdom, it was decided, once again, to move the capital. The Shang emperor called for help from its vassal state, Zhou, whose Duke agreed to send help, thus gaining the gratitude and confidence of the Shang. Later events led to mutual disaffection and distrust, and eventually to open conflict.

THE JUDGMENT

Large undertakings in particular are favored, although it is an auspicious time for all endeavors.

THE LINES

1   Initiating large-scale projects now is favored. There will be no major obstructions to your plans.

2   A show of gratitude for your good fortune is in order.

3   Responding to others' calls for assistance wins their trust.

4   Turn aside from your own path to offer aid to those in need.

5   Trust from those you have helped is a valuable reward for your services.

6   The support of allies and friends may falter. Unless your are determined to prevail through your own resources, you may fail for lack of support.

LAKE

OVER

HEAVEN

43 STRIDE

At an inquiry at the King's court,
The captives wailed,
And alarming news came from the provinces.
Do not bear arms forthwith.
Auspicious to go somewhere.

1   Injury in the toe.
Going will bring not success, but woes.

2   An alarmed cry.
There are soldiers in the night.
Fear not.

3   Injury in the face.
Misfortune.
The gentleman walks alone rapidly,
Getting wet in the rain.
Infuriating but harmless.

4   Smarting in the buttocks,
His steps are tottery.
Walking a goat in penitence,*
His words are not trusted.

5   A gazelle goes leaping down the road.
Safe and sound.

6   A dog barks.
In the end disaster comes.

*To walk a goat was a gesture of humility, used especially by a defeated commander to signify surrender.

COMMENTARY

There are dangers present everywhere, some of which are of our own making. The signs, however, are not always what they seem, and the action one takes may not always lead to the result hoped for. Thoughtful precaution is advised.

THE JUDGMENT

There is danger and bad news all about. You should eschew violent action but try to deal with the situation through diplomatic means.

THE LINES

1 When your initial steps are subverted, plunging forward would be disastrous.

2 The dangers you fear are more imaginary than real. The real foes are within and must be conquered in order to move forward.

3 Taking another stride forward results in an infuriating and humiliating experience.

4 You have been chastened and are reeling from punishment. Your public gestures of penitence are perceived as being insincere.

5 This is a note of grace in this otherwise dreary hexagram. A narrow passage of light is offered, which can bring safety and sanctuary.

6 In ancient China a dog barking in the marketplace was an omen of impending danger. This is a warning of possible harm.

HEAVEN

OVER

WIND

44 RENDEZVOUS

The girl is hurt.
Inauspicious for marriage.

1   Weaving on a golden loom.
Good omen.
Going somewhere, one sees misfortune:
A lean pig tied and dragged.

2   There is fish in the kitchen.
Faultless, but inappropriate for guests.

3   Smarting in the buttocks,
His steps are tottery.
Danger. No great woes.

4   There is no fish in the kitchen.
Making offerings brings misfortune.

5   Wrapping melon with leaves of staple grain:*
The downfall of Shang.
It brought wrath from Heaven.

6   Rendezvous in the corner.
Awkward, but blameless.

*Apparently an act of sacrilege.

COMMENTARY

We read this hexagram on many levels and simultaneously uncover a wealth of meanings that reinforce and enrich each other. There is historical reference to the Zhou people's rendezvous with destiny, in snatching the imperial throne from the Shang. The latter's downfall was attributed to the wrath of Heaven at their sacrilegious behavior (wrapping melon in leaves of grain). The hexagram also literally refers to the inappropriateness of illicit sexual liaisons in particular, and to inappropriate behavior in general. In making ancestral offerings, in entertaining guests, and in all we do, it is vital that we act in accordance with accepted moral standards.

THE JUDGMENT

There can be no meeting of the minds if both parties are not fully equal to each other and to the requirements of the situation in which they are to meet.

THE LINES

1   You are in a protected and even privileged situation; but if you step outside your golden ghetto you will see misfortune, struggle, and suffering all around you.

2   What you have is adequate for yourself but not appropriate for offering to others.

3   You are in a weakened condition as a result of some situation you created for yourself. Be careful.

4   You cannot give what you do not have.

5   Inappropriate behavior brings its own consequences. Careless and sacrilegious offerings of the Shang brought down the wrath of Heaven and cost them an empire.

6   Unnecessary meetings with inappropriate people can create awkward situations.

LAKE

OVER

EARTH

45 ILLNESS

Sign of the Sacrifice.
The King goes to the ancestral temple.
Auspicious to see the great personage.
Sign of the Sacrifice.*
Auspicious omen.
Favorable to offer big cattle.**
Auspicious to go somewhere.

1　Punishment was ordered, but not carried out.
He became confused, incoherent,
The laughingstock of the whole house.
Fear not. It is safe to go.

2　Lasting well-being. No troubles.
If there be sincerity,
Summer offering will bring good.

3　Ailing, lamenting.
Nothing can be gained.
There is no harm in going,
Only a little awkwardness.

4　Great fortune. No troubles.

5　Ailing in office.
No blame.
Rather than penalty, great fortune comes.
Regret forever disappears.

6　Offering funeral gifts in tears.
Blameless.

*"Sign of the Sacrifice" occurs twice here, indicating that the text may have been an amalgamation of two different editions.
**"Big cattle" is a whole sacrificial cow, used only on major occasions.

COMMENTARY

Illness and, by extension, adversity in general, are not without purpose. Suffering contrasts with well-being, teaching us the value and richness of abundant good health. It opens us to compassion; it teaches endurance and tests the limits of our mental and physical strength. Surviving illness gives us a dual sense of both our fragility and our courage.

THE JUDGMENT

This is deemed a good hexagram as a whole, one befitting a ritual ceremony. The moment is deemed so auspicious that one could offer "big cattle"— a whole sacrificial cow. Thus, you could successfully curry favor, and get somewhere.

THE LINES

1 Expecting ill fortune that does not materialize can be disorienting. Ridicule can be faced down.

2 Well-being is regained by having faith in oneself. Prayers will be answered only if offered in sincerity.

3 Complaints do not help an illness. In fact, things are not nearly as bad as you think. Facing your peers is awkward, but it is something you can handle.

4 Realizing the imaginary nature of your illness clears up the problem.

5 A certain amount of malaise always goes with great responsibility. It should be considered a sign of success rather than a form of punishment.

6 Expressing appropriate emotion is above criticism.

EARTH

OVER

WIND

46 ASCENDANCE

Sign of the Great Sacrifice.
See the great personage. Fear not.
Favorable for southern expedition.

1 Promotion, indeed.
   Great fortune.

2 If there be sincerity,
   Summer offering will bring good.

3 Ascending to the hill town.

4 The King offers sacrifice at Mount Qi.*
   All goes well. No troubles.

5 Good omen.
   You will go up the steps.

6 Ascending by night.
   Ceaseless striving reaps gains.

---

*King Wen was released from a Shang prison after seven years of confinement. His return to his Zhou homeland marked the beginning of a plan to overthrow the Shang Dynasty by the Zhou. It was a long and arduous undertaking, which came to fruition only after King Wen's death, through continued efforts by his son King Wu. (See Chapter 2.)

COMMENTARY

Success may come in many forms, but in this hexagram, success comes through a conscious and persistent effort of the will. Step by step, we ascend. Working night and day, ever faithful to our goals, we crown ourselves with glory.

THE JUDGMENT

It may be necessary to enlist the help of someone in a high place to achieve your goals, but the response will be favorable. You may have to undertake a significant move, but that, too, shall prove beneficial.

THE LINES

1 Your efforts are duly noted and rewarded.

2 Prayers will be answered only if sincere.

3 Your goals are lofty but attainable.

4 King Wen's sacrifices were pleasing to Heaven and his offerings were accepted.

5 You will make progress if you persist in your efforts.

6 Working night and day will bring rewards.

LAKE

OVER

WATER

47 TRAPPED

Sign of the Sacrifice.
Auspicious for the great personage.
No troubles.
The chatter has no credibility.

1 Caned in the buttocks,
Thrown into a dungeon,
Unseen for three years.

2 Sated in wine and food,
When a vermilion robe arrives.
Favorable to offer sacrifice.
To advance brings misfortune.

3 He is trapped in the crags,
Surrounded by thorns.
Entering his mansion,
One cannot find his wife.
Disaster.

4 Slow, the homeward passage.
Trapped in a golden carriage.
Difficult time. Good ending.

5 Fidget and mope.
Trapped in a vermilion robe.
Take it off, slowly.
Favorable to offer sacrifice.

6 Trapped amongst wild grass.
Trapped in a logjam.
Move and you'll regret it, some say.
But you should strike out.

COMMENTARY

One can feel trapped under many different circumstances. Even success and the trappings of power offer no protection from feelings of stagnation and despair. Whatever our situation in life—whether we ride in a golden carriage or wither away in the foulest slum—we are always free to strike out for a change. Action alone can set us free; bemoaning our fate only mires us more deeply in despair.

THE JUDGMENT

Action is a surer method of resolving problems than endless chatter, but it takes a person of mature insight and great resolve to break free from stagnant and outworn patterns.

THE LINES

1   A setback has led to stagnation.

2   The outward symbols of success must be supported by inner strength. Prayer and meditation are prerequisites of action.

3   You feel abandoned, trapped, alone. There is nowhere to turn.

4   Even those who have attained great wealth and power must struggle to overcome problems and endure difficulties. Having attained some success already avails them of greater resources in overcoming obstacles.

5   Wealth and success may become traps, suffocating and stifling the person who bears them. If this is so, the person must deliberately strip himself of these trappings in order to be really free.

6   Some will advise you to tolerate a stagnant situation, but you must take bold action to set yourself free.

WATER

OVER

WIND

48 THE WELL

Renewing the town, but not the well.
Nothing lost, nothing gained.
When overuse depletes the well,
And new ones are not dug,
You get broken pitchers.
Misfortune.

1   A muddy well: unfit for drinking.
    An old pit: No game is trapped.

2   Shooting small fish in a well.
    You get a broken, leaky pitcher.

3   The well is cleansed, but unused.
    It saddens my heart.
    Draw water from it
    To nurture my King.

4   The well is lined with tiles.
    Safe.

5   The well is clear as a cool spring.
    Drink.

6   Someone used the well
    And left the cover off.
    Impose penalties.
    Great fortune.

COMMENTARY

Wells exist in China today in the same shape and form as they did in ancient China. Generations have come and gone, each drawing from the same well, receiving nourishment from the same inexhaustible source of life-giving water. Wells are a focal point of village life and a powerful metaphor of what is essential, inexhaustible, and unchanging in the human condition. This hexagram reminds us to take care of the fundamentals of life.

THE JUDGMENT

If you try to milk a situation dry or deplete your resources, you will be creating problems for yourself.

THE LINES

1   An unproductive, unnourishing situation.

2   Taking inappropriate action creates more problems. Do not overreact.

3   You have unused talents and resources available to you that would be of great benefit to both you and others.

4   A process of renewal is taking place. There is a sense of good things to come.

5   You have the best of resources available to you, but you must avail yourself of them.

6   Careless and inappropriate action should be punished.

LAKE

OVER

FIRE

49 REVOLUTION

On the day of the public gathering
Punishments are meted out.
Sign of the Great Sacrifice.
Auspicious omen.
Regret disappears.

1 Tie it with the leather of yellow ox.*

2 On the day of the public gathering,
A new order is proclaimed.
Auspicious to take arms.
Blameless.

3 Taking arms brings disaster.
Omen of danger.
Changing one's words three times
Brings punishment.

4 Regret disappears.
Punishment ordered, and rescinded.
All goes well.

5 Changeable as a tiger is the great personage.
You don't need the oracle.
Expect punishment.

6 Changeable as a leopard is the gentleman.
Leathery is the face of the common man.
To advance brings disaster.
To settle down is favorable.

*This is a pun on the Chinese character naming this hexagram, which also means "leather."

COMMENTARY

Chinese history has seen the rise and fall of more than thirty dynasties, each ended by revolution. Just before dawn on the first day of the second moon (February), in the year 1122 B.C., King Wu of Zhou rose against the evil Emperor Jou of Shang and replaced him on the throne. The revolution had been long planned and was prudently executed. Earlier, King Wu had held a military exercise by the river Meng, where eight hundred heads of state came, urging him to move against Jou. A white fish leapt into King Wu's boat, signaling that Shang was strong (white being the color of Shang). King Wu decided that the time was not ripe, withdrew, and continued his preparation for two more years before making the fateful move.

THE JUDGMENT

Justice will be handed down publicly so that all will be aware of the fate of transgressors. This is auspicious for those who have behaved with loyalty and virtue.

THE LINES

1 Your determination must be firm and strong.

2 The intention for change is announced for all to see.

3 Wait for total readiness. There is no going back on your word.

4 Lingering doubts disappear, and so too the need for punishment.

5 Powerful people can be capricious and turn on you cruelly without cause or warning.

6 More preparation and consolidation are needed. The people have not responded to the cause because the leadership is wavering.

FIRE

OVER

WIND

50 THE CAULDRON

Great auspicious omen.
Sign of the Sacrifice.

1 The cauldron sits with upturned legs,
The better to clean the dregs.
He gets a concubine to have a son.
Blameless.

2 The cauldron is filled with food,
But my wife is not feeling good.
I am not able to go.
All's well.

3 The cauldron's ears have come apart.
It's now useless for storing lard.
The pheasant is not served.
If it rains, regret will subside.
All ends well.

4 The cauldron's legs buckle,
Spilling the Duke's victual,
Making a muddled puddle.
Disaster.

5 A yellow-eared cauldron
Hauled on a golden pole.
Auspicious omen.

6 A cauldron hauled on a jade pole.
Great fortune.
Everything goes.

COMMENTARY

Traditionally, the cauldron served two functions: It was a cooking and serving vessel (thus suggesting the idea of nourishment) and it was a ritual vessel for offering sacrifices at the ancestral temple. The unique structure of this hexagram reinforces its dual message. Each line is divided into two parts: The first conveys a vivid and concrete image, the second offers advice. We will find our lives to be well ordered only when there is harmony between the physical and metaphysical dimensions.

THE JUDGMENT

The cauldron symbolizes double good fortune: material prosperity at home and spiritual well-being in public.

THE LINES

1   It is sometimes necessary to make a clean sweep of things and to start anew. There is no fault in this.

2   In the midst of prosperity, problems can exist. Even though you feel weighed down, things are generally favorable.

3   A cauldron without its handles is no longer useful for storage or serving. If something has outlived its usefulness, discard it. Releasing your feelings will prove to be therapeutic.

4   A defective instrument can prove disastrous.

5   A cauldron carried on a golden pole signifies both the prosperity of its owner and the importance of the occasion on which it is used. Conditions are very favorable.

6   Jade is prized for its unique combination of hardness (Yang) and soft lustrousness (Yin). Its value exceeds even that of gold, and it symbolizes the best of fortunes.

THUNDER

OVER

THUNDER

51 THUNDER

Sign of the Sacrifice.
Thunder comes roaring,
'Mid laughter ringing.
A hundred miles trembling,
My goblet never spilling.

1   After the thunder came roaring,
Laughter broke out ringing.
All's well.

2   Thunder bodes danger.
Money is lost.
Climb the nine hills.
Don't chase after it.
You will get it back in seven days.

3   Threatening, threatening thunder.
It will pass.
No peril.

4   Thunder.
Falling into the mud.

5   Thunder comes, thunder goes.
Danger.
The work goes on.

6   Menacing, menacing thunder.
Look left, look right.
Thunder strikes!
It strikes not him but his neighbor.
Safe.
There is talk of marriage.

COMMENTARY

Life brings a variety of storms, and trouble may appear in many guises: natural disasters, lost wealth, humiliation, fear, and so on. Teaching us to weather storms, the Oracle's message has never been clearer: "Keep your inner sense of strength clear and steady; all things are passing, and the work goes on."

THE JUDGMENT

Keeping an inner sense of security allows you to triumph over any disaster with grace and style.

THE LINES

1 Celebration releases the tensions that accumulate under pressure.

2 You can never lose what is truly yours; it always returns in the end.

3 Dangers pass.

4 Succumbing to fear and anxiety can lead to humiliation.

5 Dangers and disasters come and go, but the work of daily life goes on.

6 Dangers may befall those closest to you while you yourself escape.

MOUNTAIN

OVER

MOUNTAIN

52 MOUNTAIN

He looks out for the back,
But not the body.
One walks his yard,
And finds him not.

1 Watching the foot.
No ills.
Lasting good omen.

2 Watching the calf.
He is not pleased
Unless it's fat.

3 Watching the waist,
The loins got hurt.
Danger.
The heart is confused.

4 Watching the body.
No ills.

5 Watching the mouth,
Speaking in order.
Regret disappears.

6 Constant watch.
All's well.

COMMENTARY

The old pictographic form of the character for the name of this hexagram consists of an eye above a person, meaning "to watch, especially a person." It is in this archaic sense that this character is used in the various lines here. We are advised not to forget the whole while concentrating on the particular. Overemphasis on minor details gives us a distorted picture and may blind us to what is really important.

THE JUDGMENT

Attention to detail may divert you from seeing things in proper perspective. You may be missing the point.

THE LINES

1 You are off to a good beginning, and that strong beginning brings with it lasting good luck.

2 You have made some progress, but not enough to satisfy you.

3 While your attention was focused on one problem, another problem arose, more serious than the first. You feel confused and upset.

4 You are safe from harm when you are mindful of all possible aspects of any given situation. When you take care of the whole, the parts automatically receive their due.

5 Be careful of what you say and to whom you say it.

6 Be constantly watchful for the first sign of trouble and act to correct it. You will do well if you are consistently careful.

WIND

OVER

MOUNTAIN

53 PROGRESS

Favorable for a maiden's marriage.
Auspicious omen.

1 The wild goose is progressing to the shore.
Danger for a youngster.
Reproach ensures safety.

2 The wild goose is progressing to the cliff.
Eat and drink in joy.
All's well.

3 The wild goose is progressing to the plateau.
The husband sets out, but will not return.
The wife conceives, but will not deliver.
Misfortune.
Guard against robbers.

4 The wild goose is progressing to the woods,
Perchance finding a log to perch on.
Safe.

5 The wild goose is progressing to the slopes.
For three years the wife would not conceive.
In the end nothing can impede her.
All goes well.

6 The wild goose is progressing to the heights.
Its feathers can be used in dance.
All's well.

COMMENTARY

This hexagram beautifully portrays for us the long and difficult progress of the wild goose in migration. Never abandoning its place in the flock's formation, the goose continues its journey, overcoming all of the setbacks and obstacles in its path. Forever faithful to its mate (never taking another, even if abandoned by death), the wild goose is also firmly committed to its place within the social order. Strengthened by this stability, the goose has the stamina and endurance to persevere. Its journey is marked by setbacks overcome, and its persistence leads eventually to the richest of triumphs.

THE JUDGMENT

The hexagram is particularly favorable for questions relating to marriage, relationships, and your place in a social organization.

THE LINES

1 As you begin any new venture, you may require the guidance and counsel of the more experienced. If you are open to allowing yourself to learn from the experience of others, you will do well.

2 It is believed that the wild goose signals its cohorts to share in whatever food it may find. It is blessed and joyous for us to share our good fortune with others.

3 Progress may be stalled by many things: being in an inappropriate place, taking rash action, overambitious plans, the envy and malice of others. No matter what shape the obstacle takes, perseverance and fidelity will, in the long run, bring progress.

4 With flexibility, you should be able to find safety and security in any situation.

5 Progress is again delayed but inevitable. Keep to your course.

6 You are about to reach the summit of success, the goal for which you have long worked. What you leave behind will have great value to others.

THUNDER

OVER

LAKE

54 THE MARRYING MAIDEN

To advance brings misfortune.
There is nothing to be gained.

1 The maiden marries,
With her younger sister as consort.*
The lameness is cured.
Auspicious to advance.

2 The blindness is cured.
Good omen for a prisoner.

3 The maiden marries,
With her elder sister as consort.
Both will be sent home.

4 The maiden's marriage is postponed.
There is time for a late marriage.

5 Emperor Yi gave his daughter in marriage.
The princess is not as beautiful as her consort.**
After the full moon, favorable.

6 The maiden holds the basket, which is empty.
The young man stabs the lamb, but draws no blood.
There is nothing to be gained.***

*See note in hexagram 11 PEACE.
**King Wen married the daughter of Emperor Yi, but her consort Taisi mothered his heir, King Wu.
(See Chapter 2.)
***This refers to a wedding custom in which the bride appears with a basket of offerings, and the
groom draws blood from a lamb. The smearing of animal blood was a ritual of consecration and
purification. (Cf. footnote in 57 WIND.)

COMMENTARY

An ancient Chinese tale of love, marriage, and court intrigue forms the background of this hexagram. Emperor Yi arranged for the marriage of his daughter to King Wen (creator of the hexagrams). In accordance with custom, the Princess went into the marriage accompanied by Taisi, one of her younger sisters, who was to serve as second consort to King Wen. It was the prettier Taisi and not the principal consort who mothered King Wen's heir. The hexagram is not an especially auspicious one, warning us of the futility of taking action. It does, however, focus on the many benefits of the married state, particularly for overcoming long-standing incapacities. By joining together, husband and wife may compensate for their individual weaknesses and overcome their disadvantages. Empty, ceremonial marriages, however, bear no fruit and bring no benefits to either party.

THE JUDGMENT

This is not a propitious time for any new undertakings. Any ventures begun now will end in frustration.

THE LINES

1 Whatever has been hindering you will be removed so that the path becomes clear and you are free to move.

2 Whatever has prevented you from seeing things clearly has been removed.

3 Your understanding will not succeed, and your efforts will be rejected.

4 There is a delay in getting what you want. Patience is advised.

5 Somebody who occupies a position of honor is not as worthy as are other people. This situation will be redressed. Those in an inferior position may rise to favor because of their innate superiority.

6 Empty rituals bring forth no benefits. This is a sterile and impotent situation.

THUNDER

OVER

FIRE

55 ABUNDANCE

Sign of the Sacrifice.
The King lends his presence.
Fear not.
Noon is the auspicious hour.

1   Meeting his hostess.
    For the next ten days, no troubles.
    Going brings rewards.

2   How expansive is the awning.
    A candle burns at noon.
    Going brings hallucinations,
    And punishment.
    Off with the awning,
    And all's well.

3   How expansive is the thatched house.
    He saw a ghost at noon,
    And broke his right arm.
    No fault.

4   How expansive is the awning.
    He saw the Dipper at noon,
    And met his good host.
    All's well.

5   He came to Shang,
    Receiving gifts and praise.
    All's well.

6   How expansive is the house.
    An awning covers the yard.
    He peers into the door,
    And sees not a soul.
    For three years no one is seen.
    Disaster.

COMMENTARY

An ambassador from the court of the Zhou to the Shang capital encounters great material splendor in the midst of spiritual malaise and isolation. The images used are graphic and vividly portray a stark loneliness and inner terror.

THE JUDGMENT

After the fullness of light at noon, the day begins to turn to shadows. It is a good time to pay homage to Heaven in the presence of those who represent the power and authority of the state.

THE LINES

1   It is a good time to act, and support is available for your undertakings.

2   Luxury is impressive but unnecessary. Extravagant gestures (burning a candle at noon) can lead to a distorted sense of reality, and this, in turn, can create fearful inner visions that bring with them their own form of punishment.

3   Fears materializing in the shape of inner dreams can lead to trauma and even temporary incapacity, but you are not to blame.

4   Darkening the brilliance of the sky enables us to see evening stars at midday. Wealth and technology can turn day to night. The situation is favorable.

5   Your presence and your ideas are well received.

6   Loneliness can exist in the midst of great splendor.

FIRE

OVER

MOUNTAIN

56 THE TRAVELER

Sign of the Small Sacrifice.
Auspicious for the traveler.

I Little, little traveler,
Leaves his house to wander,
Courting disaster.

2 The traveler takes lodging,
Money stashed in his clothing.
He gets a servant.
All goes well.

3 The traveler's inn is burning,
The servant is sent scurrying.
Danger.

4 The traveler builds his own quarters.
The lost sum he recovers.
But his heart is not glad.

5 He shoots at a pheasant,
Losing an arrow.
In the end this brings renown.

6 A bird's nest is burning.
The traveler first laughs, then weeps.
He lost his oxen at the Kingdom of Yi.*
Disaster.

*This hexagram is a pure narrative of the story of the adventurous Prince Hai, an early forebear of the Shang people who traveled to the Kingdom of Yi to raise cattle and invented the ox yoke while there. He was the target of conspiracies, and he suffered a series of setbacks: He lost his herd of sheep; he narrowly escaped death at the hands of an unknown arsonist, thanks to a mysterious rap on his bed that had roused him. But eventually his luck ran out. The local king, who had had an eye on his yoked oxen all along, killed him and took his flock. (See Chapter 2.)

COMMENTARY

On some level of being we are all travelers and seekers, restlessly pursuing a better life (job, relationship, experience), which always looms tantalizingly just beyond a glimpsed horizon. Every step of our journey carries risk as well as promise, and though we have support in our efforts, we must face our destiny alone. It is essentially our own task to build our shelter, to save ourselves from peril. These tasks are lonely and difficult and, although necessary, they do not fulfill the heart of one who is always focused on the obtainable. It is the pursuit alone that brings glory to the traveler.

THE JUDGMENT

The lesson of Prince Hai should prove helpful for one embarking on a new venture.

THE LINES

1 You feel so small and frail as you venture out into the wide, wide world, where there are challenges and excitement, but also risks and real dangers.

2 Well under way, you have the wherewithal to secure the services of able assistants.

3 You may be trapped and endangered by hidden enemies, but you will eventually find a route to safety.

4 You have recovered from losses, although the unpleasant experience leaves you anxious.

5 You aimed to acquire the unobtainable pheasant, symbol of personal transcendence and immortality. Although the pursuit uses up valuable resources, and fails, you earned admiration for the style and quality of the quest.

6 There is danger to home and possessions. If you let your guard down, you will lose all.

WIND

OVER

WIND

57 WIND

Sign of the Small Sacrifice.
Auspicious to go somewhere.
Auspicious to see the great personage.

1 Advance or retreat?
For the soldier, either bodes well.

2 Crouching under the bed.
The shaman smears blood on you.*
All's well.
No ills.

3 Crouching and frowning.
Troubled.

4 Regret disappears.
Bagging three kinds of game at the hunt.

5 Good omen.
Regret disappears.
Everything goes well.
A poor beginning gives way to a good ending.
Auspicious,
Three days before the seventh,
Three after the seventh.

6 Crouching under the bed.
The travel money is lost.
Misfortune.

*The smearing of animal blood, followed by bathing, was a ritual of consecration and purification, performed by an official shaman. For example, when Lord Tang, founder of the Shang Dynasty, plucked the talented Iyun from total obscurity to become his prime minister, he performed this ceremony on him at the ancestral temple to expunge him of his humble past.

COMMENTARY

The Chinese character for the name of this hexagram also means "to crouch." Allowing fears and self-doubt to control our actions impedes our ability to make progress, just as crouching never gets us anywhere. A ritual cleansing is indicated, to clear out our regrets and doubts and dispel our most hidden fears.

THE JUDGMENT Realistic goals will be accomplished easily. You will receive the support you seek.

THE LINES 1 When you are in command of the situation, any specific action you take will have its own rewards.

2 Inner woes present no grave danger, but help is at hand. You would do well to consult with healers of the psyche, be it priests, psychics, or psychiatrists, to help you overcome your problems.

3 Self-doubt, hesitation, and fear will lead to inaction. You are putting yourself at risk. Beware.

4 Inner conflict is resolved. Guilt, confusion, and anxiety disappear. Great success is achieved.

5 After a faulty start, necessary corrections are made and all ends well. Make decisions with great deliberation and subject them to careful scrutiny.

6 If you are mired by fears and doubts, you can't go forward.

LAKE

OVER

LAKE

58 LAKE

Sign of the Sacrifice.
Auspicious omen.

1 Gentle talk.
All goes well.

2 Sincere talk.
All goes well.
Regret disappears.

3 Excessive talk.
Misfortune.

4 The discussion is unfinished.
The itching ailment will heal.

5 Punishing the downtrodden.
Peril.

6 Straight talk.

COMMENTARY

The Chinese character depicting this hexagram can also be translated as "talking." The message is clear and staightforward: Gentle, sincere, and honest talk produces harmony; excessive or repressive talk brings misfortune.

THE JUDGMENT

This is a good moment for communicating your deepest thoughts.

THE LINES

1 Speaking softly and sympathetically makes you heard and heeded.

2 Speaking from the heart enables you to communicate with others without misunderstanding.

3 Talking too much can lead to trouble.

4 There is much more to be said before the issue is resolved. Dissatisfactions will be alleviated.

5 It is dangerous to push the abused too far. Curb your demands.

6 Above all, honesty.

WIND

OVER

WATER

59 FLOWING

The King goes to the temple.
Auspicious to cross the great stream.
Auspicious omen.

	1	Auspicious to castrate a horse. It will be strong.
	2	Water washes over the stall. Regret disappears.
	3	Water laves the body. No regrets.
	4	Water sprays the crowd. Great auspicious omen. Water laps at the hillside. You cannot imagine what will happen.
	5	Sweating profusely, Wailing loudly. Water laps at the King's house. It's safe.
	6	Bleeding profusely. Leave, go far away, and be safe.

COMMENTARY

Flowing water, delightful when it is gentle, but menacing when it grows to a torrent, had a special meaning for the ancient Chinese. On the one hand, it was associated with spiritual renewal, as emphasized by the famous maxim inscribed on the bronze bath basin of Lord Tang, founder of the Shang dynasty: "Renew youself today, and another day, and each and every day." On the other hand, it was a fearsome force of destruction: Eight times during the six centuries of Shang rule, floods forced the moving of the capital.

The images of flowing water that dominate this hexagram vividly convey to us both the delights and benefits of gently flowing water and the fearsome destructiveness of a deluge. Nevertheless, even when it expresses fear, the hexagram holds out the hope of safe passage.

THE JUDGMENT

This is a favorable time for going places, consulting those with power and expertise; a good time for getting things done.

THE LINES

1 This is an excellent opportunity for protecting your vital assets.

2 Water rises, washing away accumulations of dirt and sediment.

3 Bathing in flowing water gives a feeling of spiritual refreshment.

4 The flow of water quickens. An initial sense of fun and excitement gives way to anxious apprehension.

5 The flow has become a flood, and there is chaos and confusion. Stability is threatened, but you will weather the danger.

6 In the aftermath of the flood, there are injuries and destruction everywhere. It would be wise to leave and start over somewhere else.

WATER

OVER

LAKE

60 FRUGALITY

Sign of the Sacrifice.
If frugality be hardship,
There is no fortune.

1 Not stepping out of the courtyard.
No troubles.

2 Not stepping out of the front gate.
Misfortune.

3 Not saving now,
Lamenting later.

4 Content in frugality.
Sign of the Sacrifice.

5 Enjoying frugality.
To go brings rewards.

6 Frugality as hardship.
Omen of misfortune.

COMMENTARY

One of the most necessary and enduring virtues of the Chinese people has been frugality. Hexagram 60 celebrates the vitality of this virtue and admonishes us to see in its practice an opportunity for contentment and good fortune. We must learn to live within imposed limitations and be comfortable with what we have.

THE JUDGMENT

Your attitude determines how much of life you enjoy. If you are not content with what you already have, you cannot fully enjoy the fortune that is yours for the taking.

THE LINES

1 Observing the natural constraints inherent in your situation frees you of problems.

2 If the moment is right, then it is necessary to take action. Hesitation, doubt, and delay would be harmful.

3 Failing to provide resources for the future can result in deprivation, humiliation, and hardship.

4 Living contentedly within the bounds you have set for yourself brings the blessings of Heaven.

5 You can actually grow to enjoy a frugal lifestyle. Living on a modest scale frees resources for other productive efforts.

6 Seeing frugality as a difficult and tiresome burden creates a bitter emotional climate that invites failure and suffering.

WIND

OVER

LAKE

61 SINCERITY

In sincerity,
Humble gifts are well received.
Auspicious to cross the great stream.
Auspicious omen.

1 Enjoying peace.
  Peril intrudes.

2 An egret sings in the shade,
  Its young harmonizing.
  I have a good wine
  For you to share.

3 The enemy is ours.
  Some feel elated, others tired.
  Some are weeping, others singing.

4 After the full moon,
  Horses go astray.
  No fault.

5 Punished by imprisonment.
  No peril.

6 A chicken flies to the sky.
  Omen of disaster.

COMMENTARY

Sincerity, or the lack of it, is expressed in various ways in this hexagram. It refers to sincerity in sharing among friends. It describes the venting of true feelings at a moment of victory. It implies that with sincerity no harm will come to us, and the lack of it will surely lead to disaster.

THE JUDGMENT

Sincere prayers will be answered, even though you can afford to make only meager offerings.

THE LINES

1   Such is the nature of the world that your peace can be shattered by events beyond your control.

2   The bond between good friends is expressed here through a quatrain very much in the style of folk poetry of the time. The image of egrets singing in harmony sets a mood for the main theme.

3   People can react differently to the same situation, even a seemingly clear-cut one, such as victory over an enemy. You should voice your feelings sincerely.

4   A recurring reassurance in the I Ching, this promises that what is truly yours cannot be lost.

5   A sincere person need not fear punishment.

6   Disaster will befall the insincere and pretentious.

THUNDER

OVER

MOUNTAIN

62 SMALL EXCESS

Sign of the Sacrifice.
Auspicious omen.
Attempt the small, not the big.
A flying bird leaves a message:
Go not high, but low.
Great fortune.

1   A bird flies with an arrow in it.
    Misfortune.

2   Overtaking the grandfather,
    He encounters the father.
    Trailing the King,
    He encounters the Minister.
    No fault.

3   Guard against excesses beforehand.
    Indulgence could mean destruction.
    Misfortune.

4   No troubles.
    Stop excesses beforehand.
    Danger must be warned against.
    Do not take long-term action.

5   Thick clouds and no rain,
    From my west field cometh.
    The Duke went shooting,
    And got the bird in a cave.

6   Abetting excess.
    A net is set for a flying bird.
    Misfortune.
    A disaster indeed.

COMMENTARY

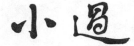

We are gently admonished to curtail our ambitions and engage only in activities in which we are competent. Even if we lack the requisite inner resources for greatness, we may nonetheless enjoy success in modest endeavors.

THE JUDGMENT You should be modest and cautious and pay heed to your natural limitations.

THE LINES 1 Going ahead while you are incapacitated brings misfortune.

2 Disappointment in failing to make contact with superiors need not convey a sense of guilt.

3 Self-discipline can protect you from overindulgence, which could otherwise be your downfall. Do not allow things to get out of hand.

4 Cautious and controlled behavior safeguards against the dangers of willful and impetuous conduct. Prudence prevents later regrets.

5 In a mood of anxious expectation, you score a small success.

6 Encouraging excesses is tantamount to setting a trap for someone and will surely end in disaster.

WATER

OVER

FIRE

63 FULFILLMENT

Sign of the Sacrifice.
Auspicious in small things.
Good beginning, chaotic ending.

1   He lifted the front tip of his sash,
    And the tail got wet.
    No harm done.

2   The woman lost her wig.
    Seek not.
    It will be found in seven days.

3   King Wu Ding warred against Devil's Land,*
    And conquered it in three years.
    Use not common people.

4   The quilt got wet.
    Be alert all day.

5   The eastern neighbor's lavish sacrifice
    Falls short of the western neighbor's simple rite.
    Substance counts.**

6   The head got wet.
    Danger.

*Wu Ding was a king of Shang. (See Chapter 2.)
**The eastern neighbor refers to Shang, and the western neighbor to Zhou.

COMMENTARY

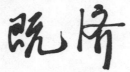

The literal meaning of the two Chinese characters naming this hexagram is "already across (a river)." It simultaneously conveys a sense of joyous completion and a release from the tension and anxiety of the crossing. It is in keeping with the philosophy of the I Ching that FULFILLMENT does not complete the cycle of hexagrams.

Fulfillment brings us to that brief moment when all the forces of nature are in harmony, when energies are poised in perfect balance. This moment of completion is also a turning point and a moment of disintegration, when energy begins to disperse and dissonance resounds. We are called again to review the struggle, gather up the fragments, and begin anew the never-ending effort to restore peace, order, harmony once more.

THE JUDGMENT

This hexagram is favorable for small and modest efforts, but does not favor ambitious programs. Things start off strongly but may end poorly. The tide is turning, and although conditions seem favorable for the moment, there are problems in store.

THE LINES

1   You find that you cannot handle everything at once; things are beginning to be too much for you, but this is not a problem yet.

2   Do not waste time on vainglorious matters. Attend to your proper affairs and you will get what is due.

3   The Shang emperor Wu Ding was successful in his campaign to subdue a "barbarian" state because he used a highly skilled general. Be careful to employ people of superior talents and motivations.

4   A wet blanket not only offers no warmth but dampens all it touches. Be careful.

5   Intent is important when making ritual offerings. A simple sacrifice offered with real devotion is more effective than an elaborate ritual without faith or feeling.

6   You have gotten in over your head, and the situation is dangerous.

FIRE

OVER

WATER

64 UNFULFILLMENT

Sign of the Sacrifice.
A little fox, crossing at the shallow,
Got its tail wet.
There is nothing to be gained.

I   The tail got wet.
    Awkward.

2   He lifted the front tip of his sash.
    Good omen.

3   You are not across yet.
    To advance brings misfortune.
    Inauspicious to cross the great stream.

4   Good omen. Regret disappears.
    Zhen led against Devil's Land.*
    In three years he was rewarded
    In the Great Kingdom.**

5   Good omen. Regret disappears.
    The gentleman's goblet holds the penalty.***

6   A penalty drink.
    No fault.
    His head got wet:
    Punishment for missteps.

*Zhen was a general from the state of Zhou on loan to King Wu Ding of Shang. (See 63 FULFILLMENT.)
**The Great Kingdom refers to Shang.
***See note in 5 WAITING.

COMMENTARY

The two Chinese characters naming this hexagram literally mean "not yet across (a river)." Thus the cycle of hexagrams ends, not on a note of completion, but at the beginning of an endeavor. We are warned against the bravado of overconfidence by a proverbial little fox (the wise old fox is a symbol of wily caution). Plunging into projects in a headlong way can have a dampening effect on pride. Historically, the hexagram relates the story of General Zhen from the Zhou state, who was sent on loan to assist the Shang Dynasty in their endless provincial wars against neighboring "barbarians."

THE JUDGMENT Overconfident and brash behavior results in frustration and humiliation. There is no advantage to pushing ahead if the moment is not auspicious.

THE LINES 1 Falling flat on your face is embarrassing, but there is no real danger.

2 Taking small precautions can protect against large mistakes.

3 This is not the time to forge ahead with your plans.

4 When the time and place is right, bold action brings great rewards.

5 The time is right, and the moment shining with good fortune. Pay your debts, abandon the past, and look to the future.

6 Overexuberance or intemperance violates the spirit of celebration and results in chastisement.

APPENDIX

LIST OF TRIGRAMS

NUMBER	NAME	SYMBOL	CHINESE NAME
1	Heaven	☰	乾 Qian
2	Earth	☷	坤 Kun
3	Thunder	☳	震 Zhen
4	Water	☵	坎 Kan
5	Mountain	☶	艮 Gen
6	Wind	☴	巽 Xun
7	Fire	☲	離 Li
8	Lake	☱	兌 Dui

MATRIX OF HEXAGRAM NUMBERS

Go to the column under the upper trigram. Read down until you reach the row marked by the lower trigram.

LOWER \ UPPER	1	2	3	4	5	6	7	8
1	1	11	34	5	26	9	14	43
2	12	2	16	8	23	20	35	45
3	25	24	51	3	27	42	21	17
4	6	7	40	29	4	59	64	47
5	33	15	62	39	52	53	56	31
6	44	46	32	48	18	57	50	28
7	13	36	55	63	22	37	30	49
8	10	19	54	60	41	61	38	58

LIST OF HEXAGRAMS

SYMBOL gives the hexagram lines in ascending order, reading left to right, with Yin represented by 0 and Yang by 1.

CODE is composed of upper and lower trigram numbers:

1 Heaven	2 Earth	3 Thunder	4 Water
5 Mountain	6 Wind	7 Fire	8 Lake

NUMBER	NAME	SYMBOL	CODE	CHINESE NAME	
1	Heaven	111111	11	乾	Qian
2	Earth	000000	22	坤	Kun
3	Retrenchment	100010	43	屯	Tun
4	Blindness	010001	54	蒙	Meng
5	Waiting	111010	41	需	Xu
6	The Court	010111	14	訟	Song
7	The Army	010000	24	師	Shi
8	Support	000010	42	比	Bi
9	Small Cattle	111011	61	小畜	Xiao Chu
10	Treading	110111	18	履	Lu
11	Peace	111000	11	泰	Tai
12	Obstruction	000111	12	否	Pi
13	Gathering	101111	17	同人	Tong Ren
14	Great Harvest	111101	71	大有	Da You
15	Modesty	001000	25	謙	Qian
16	Weariness	000100	32	豫	Yu
17	The Chase	100110	83	隨	Sui
18	Work	011001	18	蠱	Gu
19	Prevailing	110000	28	臨	Lin
20	View	000011	62	觀	Guan
21	Biting	101001	57	噬嗑	Shi Ke
22	Decoration	100101	73	賁	Ben
23	Loss	000001	52	剝	Bo
24	Return	100000	23	復	Fu
25	Propriety	100111	13	無妄	Wu Wang
26	Big Cattle	111001	51	大畜	Da Chu
27	The Cheeks	100001	53	頤	Yi
28	Great Excess	011110	86	大過	Da Guo

NUMBER	NAME	SYMBOL	CODE	CHINESE NAME	
29	Water	010010	44	坎	Kan
30	Fire	101101	77	離	Li
31	Cutting	001110	85	咸	Xian
32	Steadfastness	011100	36	恒	Heng
33	The Little Pig	001111	15	遯	Tun
34	Great Injury	111100	31	大壯	Da Zhuang
35	Advance	000101	72	晋	Jin
36	The Crying Pheasant	101000	27	明夷	Ming Yi
37	The Family	101011	67	家人	Jia Ren
38	Abandoned	110101	78	睽	Kui
39	Admonishment	001010	45	蹇	Jian
40	Letting Loose	010100	34	解	Jie
41	Decrease	110001	58	損	Sun
42	Increase	100011	63	益	Yi
43	Stride	111110	81	夬	Guai
44	Rendezvous	011111	16	姤	Hou
45	Illness	000110	82	萃	Cui
46	Ascendance	011000	26	升	Sheng
47	Trapped	010110	84	困	Kun
48	The Well	011010	46	井	Jing
49	Revolution	101110	87	革	Ge
50	The Cauldron	011101	76	鼎	Ding
51	Thunder	100100	33	震	Zhen
52	Mountain	011011	55	艮	Gen
53	Progress	001011	65	漸	Jian
54	The Marrying Maiden	110100	38	歸妹	Gui Mei
55	Abundance	101100	37	豐	Feng
56	The Traveler	001101	75	旅	Lu
57	Wind	011011	66	巽	Xun
58	Lake	110110	88	兌	Dui
59	Flowing	010011	64	渙	Huan
60	Frugality	110010	48	節	Jie
61	Sincerity	110011	68	中季	Zhong Fu
62	Small Excess	001100	35	小過	Xiao Guo
63	Fulfillment	101010	47	既濟	Ji Ji
64	Unfulfillment	010101	74	未濟	Wei Ji

INDEX OF HEXAGRAMS

NUMBER   denotes hexagram number.

CODE   is composed of upper and lower trigram numbers:

1 Heaven	2 Earth	3 Thunder	4 Water
5 Mountain	6 Wind	7 Fire	8 Lake

NAME	NUMBER	CODE	PAGE
Increase	42	63	154
Lake	58	88	186
Letting Loose	40	34	150
Little Pig, The	33	15	136
Loss	23	52	116
Marrying Maiden, The	54	38	178
Modesty	15	25	100
Mountain	52	55	174
Obstruction	12	12	94
Peace	11	21	92
Prevailing	19	28	108
Progress	53	65	176
Propriety	25	13	120
Rendezvous	44	16	158
Retrenchment	3	43	76
Return	24	23	118
Revolution	49	87	168
Sincerity	61	68	192
Small Cattle	9	61	88
Small Excess	62	35	194
Steadfastness	32	36	134
Stride	43	81	156
Support	8	42	86
Thunder	51	33	172
Trapped	47	84	164
Traveler, The	56	75	182
Treading	10	18	90
Unfulfillment	64	74	198
View	20	62	110
Waiting	5	41	80
Water	29	44	128
Weariness	16	32	102
Well, The	48	46	166
Wind	57	66	184
Work	18	56	106